THE Happy HOME

The Ultimate Guide to Creating
a Home that Brings You Joy

CHELSEA FOY
CREATOR OF *LOVELY INDEED*

SASQUATCH BOOKS
SEATTLE

KEYS
WALLET
PHONE

Contents

vii   **Foreword by Joy Cho**

ix   **Happiness Begins at Home**

1   UPLIFT

29   CALM

53   ENERGIZE

81   COMFORT

107   EMPOWER

131   EXPRESS

155   Wrapping Up

156   Acknowledgments

158   Sources

159   Index

Foreword

I started my design business and blog (both called Oh Joy!) back in 2005, in what feels like a century ago in social media years. For me, Oh Joy! grew gradually over the course of time from a design business to a lifestyle brand that includes content, products, books, and more. One theme that runs through all my work is the idea of bringing joy to the everyday. So I'm always a fan of others who also love leading the way with joy.

For over a decade, I have known Chelsea as a fellow blogger, creator, and businessperson in this weird world of social media that we somehow got into. The thing I love about Chelsea and her work is that it's not just about a pretty picture, getting likes, or making something just to make it. For her, projects, decor, and the things she surrounds herself with have meaning and intention. She always asks: How will this help make our lives better, happier, and more joyful? I couldn't be more proud of Chelsea and all the things she's accomplished since we first met so many years ago. She is truly helping others find a more joyful life.

This book is a guide to instilling the joy into your home that we all need. It's full of her ingenious tips, thought starters for making your home more joyful, lists of must-haves for various spaces in your home, easy-to-understand and joyful DIYs, prompts to help inspire a happy home, and so much more.

Enjoy!

—**JOY CHO**, founder of Oh Joy!

Happiness Begins at Home

Joy is not difficult or expensive. It's not exclusive or elusive. It's everywhere, and there's plenty to go around.

When I was a kid, my bedroom was in a constant state of flux. I used to have a habit of closing the door, telling my mom not to come in until lunchtime, and completely rearranging the room, furniture and all. My little ten-year-old muscles would push the desk across the room, place the dresser under a different window, pull down all of my posters and make new art, and arrange little vignettes of my favorite toys on the windowsill. And when it was *just so*, I would call in my mom and invite her to sit down and look at it all. To enjoy the new experience.

I remember her being generous with attentive comments (*Ah! And why did you choose to put that there? How interesting. This area with your beanbag feels very cozy.*) and ever patient as she would inevitably come in the next time to find another new arrangement. But I wasn't rearranging things to impress her or anyone else. I loved the act of changing my room because it was a way that I could make my space feel completely new and unique. I had power over my little realm, and I could wield that power to make my room feel like me. It was an act of creativity, of expression, of empowerment, of self-care. And it felt good. It made me *happy*.

Now, as an adult who has lived in fourteen different homes, things aren't that much different. I still find constant joy in creating a home that feels good. I have long believed that there is loveliness and joy in the world, accessible to us all, just waiting to be discovered or created. There's nowhere more important to create that joy than in our homes— where we eat, sleep, raise our babies, nurture our relationships, and more. As the world shifts and we are utilizing our homes for work, play, and everything in between, I do my best to maximize the joy, beauty, and functionality of my home through projects and ideas that are not just beautiful but also useful and easy to create. I may not be a plucky ten-year-old anymore, rearranging furniture, but that instinct to create a happy nest is still within me. And these days when I invite people into my home, I'm met with questions like: "How did you make that?!" "How do you make it feel so cozy in here?" "Can you come over and tell me what to do in my house?"

The answer to that last one is tricky, and not just because designing someone else's home actually sounds like my worst nightmare. The truth is, I would never presume to tell someone else how to decorate or organize their home because our spaces are such a unique reflection of our individuality. I would, however, help a friend explore and discover the things that she truly loves and values and figure out how to infuse her home with those discoveries. And that's what this book is all about.

It feels important to say that this isn't a DIY book, nor is it a book about home decor or design. At its heart, this book will show you that you have the power in your own two hands, no matter your skill set, to create a home in which you absolutely thrive. Parts of it are a celebration of making and creativity, and how those things connect us to our homes and ourselves. Making something that you can use and enjoy in your home can be a great source of joy and pride; there is a magic in making that enhances a home and the people in it. Other parts of this book are an exploration of yourself and your relationship to your home, which is a partnership that's often overlooked. I hope the ideas and prompts help you find a clear understanding of the things that matter to you and to the people who live in your space. And by the end, you'll be armed with simple tricks and ideas to create the home you've always imagined for yourself.

Each chapter is designed to help you create and lean into a different feeling within your home. It doesn't matter whether your home is a dorm room, a 350-square-foot apartment in a big city, or a sprawling farmhouse on a ranch—every space (and the rooms within it) holds a wide spectrum of feelings, from peaceful to empowering to uplifting and more. As you make your way through the chapters, take notice of the parts that resonate with you and your home. You'll start to feel the stories that you want to tell in your space coming to the surface, ready to be told.

To be clear, this isn't about running out to buy the newest home decor item that's gracing the shelves at everybody's favorite big-box store. It's not about having the latest and greatest trend splashed on your walls, and it certainly isn't about following a prescribed path to happiness in your home.

Nope. None of that. Creating a home that feels joyful is about deeper work. It's about knowing yourself: what moves you, what comforts you, what uplifts you, and where you want to land at the end of a long day. It's about knowing your home: how it supports you, how it challenges you, and where it needs you to love it. And it's about putting in time together—you, your family, your friends, and your space. Then you'll truly start to understand the ins and outs of why your home feels the way it does.

I believe that joy is found in the little moments surrounding us every day. This book has the power to guide you toward those moments of joy in your home and spin them into something beautiful. I also know that happiness is not only a state of mind but also a state of action. I hope these ideas help move you into that state of action as you create your very own happy home.

TOOLBOX

Every home needs a stash of household workhorses. I consider these my secret weapons; the tools and tricks that I keep up my sleeve to fix things in a pinch. Every one of these items is tested, tried, and true in our house, and every one of them serves multiple purposes. What's in your toolbox?

COMMAND STRIPS AND HOOKS. Command makes a huge variety of adhesive strips, hooks, picture hangers, decor holders, and more. They don't damage walls and are extremely easy to apply and remove, even after years of adhesion. I use Command Strips for everything: party decor, hanging pictures, holiday decorations, wreaths, organization, and more.

GLUE GUN. It's truly a marvel what you can do with a glue gun! Keep one handy, along with a selection of glue sticks. They're perfect for quick fixes or major DIY projects. If you have young kids, consider a low-temperature glue gun, which does the same job but doesn't get quite as hot, so it helps protect little hands from burns.

MAGIC ERASER. There are certain surfaces in a home that just hang on to grime or residue when wiped with a regular cloth. A Magic Eraser is usually great for these spots. It's also great for removing sticker residue, cleaning sneakers, removing nail polish stains, spot cleaning walls, and more. Just don't use it on delicate surfaces, and be sure to perform a spot test before you try it on anything new.

LEMON ESSENTIAL OIL. We'll talk about oils a bit more (see page 61), but if I were to recommend keeping just one around, it would be lemon. Many people use essential oils for health purposes, but lemon essential oil is a multipurpose workhorse to have on hand. Use it to remove sticky residues, get gum out of hair, remove temporary tattoos from kids' skin, and lots more. Handle with care, and refer to page 64 for safety information.

E6000. E6000 is the holy grail of adhesives. I discovered it for a crafting project years ago and never looked back (it has completely replaced Super Glue in our household). It creates an extremely strong bond but dries with a bit of flexibility, which is great for projects around the house, DIYs and crafts, and even fixing broken toys.

DRILL. Even if you're not "handy," keeping a basic drill in your toolbox is a life saver. Save your wrists and arms if you're working on a home improvement project with an electric drill instead of a screwdriver. You can even get a brush attachment and use it to clean tubs and showers, instead of scrubbing over and over.

QUALITY SCISSORS. It may seem like a no-brainer, but a good pair of scissors makes your projects so much more enjoyable and successful. Get scissors that are made for your specific use—fabric shears for sewing, snippers for gardening, or just a sharp, fresh pair of office scissors for standard home use.

MEASURING TAPE. Get yourself a great measuring tape with handy features like a lock and a belt clip. A quality measuring tape will stay with you forever and aid in hundreds of projects around the house.

Uplift

It might seem natural to assume that the living room is the heart of a home. But if the living room is the heart, the kitchen is the soul. This magical space isn't just a home for all of our cold, metallic appliances and cabinets filled with forgotten cans of soup. The kitchen, on the contrary, is where the nourishment comes from.

It's where we stand over the stove, stirring chicken soup for our sick kids. It's where we burn the first batch of cookies that we're baking for our new neighbors (and nail the second batch). And it's where we wind up at the end of the party, sitting on the counters among piles of dishes, having the deepest, best conversations while we finish the last bottle of wine.

This is a place where we nourish not just our bodies but also our relationships, our spirits, and our hearts. It lifts us up as we make a cup of coffee for a friend and sit down at the table for a chat. The kitchen holds space for us as we sit and lovingly (perhaps exhaustedly) plan a week of meals for our family. We bake a cake to brighten a neighbor's day, and the kitchen brightens our day in return.

In my home, the kitchen is a noisy and bustling place. It's school lunches in the morning and slow cookers all day; it's mismatched bowls and sticky lemons on the counter while the kids make lemonade. But among all of that surface chaos, I know that I personally enjoy a kitchen that's designed to be very functional and support our busy family.

When we were remodeling our home, it was clear to us that our narrow and dark galley kitchen was one of the first rooms we wanted to lighten and brighten, to create a more uplifting space. We knocked down a wall and opened the room up to include an airy space over the stove with a counter opposite, where the kids could do homework or guests could enjoy a drink while we cooked. We included long-term items like tile, flooring, and cabinets that were very neutral so that we could add wild pops of pattern or color like our bold tropical wallpaper (and change these things out easily and affordably).

But a room—*any* room—doesn't need a complete remodel to feel fresh and uplifting! All that it needs are the things that *you* find necessary, functional, happy, and fulfilling. This chapter is filled with ideas both large and small to help you infuse the rooms in your home with joy. And treating your senses to these small changes can bring about a major shift in the way you feel about your space.

At the end of the day, perhaps you end up in the kitchen like we do—cooking dinner, washing dishes, putting food away. But no matter which room you end up in, they can all be spaces that support you, bring joy, and uplift you every day.

Your turn! Let's talk about your own dwelling and the areas that could use an infusion of cheer. Consider your own home, including everything from the things you love and make you feel wonderful to the things that might bum you out every time you see or use them. Respond to these prompts in a journal and see where your thoughts lead.

FUNCTION

· Which room in your home is the easiest to exist in? What makes it easy? How does it feel to be in that room?

· Which room in your home is challenging? In what ways?

· Where do you go in your home when you want to feel cheerful, bright, or uplifted? What brings you to this space?

· Is there a home that you walk into and immediately feel uplifted? Whose home is it? What do you think creates those feelings?

FORM

· What types of sensory input make you feel uplifted: smell, taste, touch, sound, sight? A mix of a few of them?

· If you could teleport right now to anywhere in the world, where would it be?

  - Why?

  - What does it look like there?

  - How do you feel there?

  - How could you infuse that feeling into a space in your home?

- What would an "uplifting" home mean for you?
- Scour your memory banks for some of your very favorite belongings. Go back as far as you can! Stuffed animals, tchotchkes, sweaters, art, souvenirs—anything. Jot them down and see what they have in common, if anything. Do you see any similarities, differences, or patterns?

Now that you've spent some time with these questions, review your responses to see where they lead. Choose an uplifting project from this chapter to infuse some brightness and joy into one of your spaces. Enjoy the process!

Forage Bouquets

Having fresh flowers on a clean countertop sets off a deep and bright joy inside me. It brings up a blurry memory of my mom wiping down countertops and setting a small and simple bouquet there, fussing with the flowers until they were just so. It's spendy to keep fresh flowers on your counter all the time. But we'll often go out to the backyard or around the neighborhood and see what we can forage to create a pretty little arrangement, which is totally free. Chances are you'll have some neighbors like ours who won't mind sharing a bloom or two with you.

YOU'LL NEED:

- Foraged flowers, botanicals, leaves, or branches
- Trimming shears or strong scissors
- Container or vessel

HOW TO:

1 Start in your own backyard! Look around for sprigs, branches, or blooms that would look pretty together. These can be clippings from an herb, a small tree branch with blossoms, a flower, leaves—just about anything.
2 If you walk around the neighborhood to forage more plants, be sure to ask permission before you clip anything.
3 When you make a cut, place the shears about an inch from the bottom of a main stem or branch. Cut at a 45-degree angle, which allows for optimum water intake for the plant.
4 Place the cuttings in a vessel with water and enjoy.
5 Change the water every two to three days to keep flowers fresh longer.

Homemade Cut-Plant Preservative

Extend the life of your cut-flower bouquets with this simple recipe, added to one quart of water.

- 1 teaspoon sugar
- 1 teaspoon lemon juice or white vinegar
- ½ teaspoon household bleach

Stock Your Home Bar

What I love most about being known as the house on the block with the great cocktails is not the cocktail itself—it's the companionship. It's asking about each other's days while we squeeze the limes or hearing the clink of the ice cut through the laughter of friends. These moments add bright spots to our day and lift our spirits (no pun intended).

We keep our home bar stocked with a basic supply of items that can cover every base, should the neighbors swing by for a chat. Here's how you can do the same.

LIQUOR. If you're stocking a home bar for the first time, I recommend testing the waters with various mid-range liquors (with regard to both price and quality). If you're planning on mainly making mixed drinks or cocktails, unnecessarily high-end bottles will only bust your budget. If you plan on drinking any liquor neat or on the rocks without mixers, then it might be worth investing in something a bit more special. I recommend keeping a basic selection on hand of vodka, gin, rum (dark and light), tequila, and bourbon whiskey. Lean into what you like.

BEER, WINE, AND BUBBLES. Keep a small selection of each of these on hand, especially if you enjoy entertaining. A nice array might consist of one bottle each of red wine, white wine, prosecco, champagne, and a fun six-pack of craft beer. Once you start to learn what you or your guests enjoy, you can build your collection.

MIXERS AND GARNISHES. Stock your home bar with a simple list of basic items that you can mix and match to make a wide variety of cocktails.

GARNISHES CAN INCLUDE:

- limes
- lemons
- salt
- pepper
- Tabasco
- sugar cubes
- cocktail olives and onions

MIXERS TO KEEP HANDY INCLUDE:

- club soda
- tonic
- ginger beer
- cola
- lemon-lime soda
- fruit juices
- bitters

NOTE: If you're entertaining, don't forget to stock up on ice!

BARWARE. When it comes to barware, keep it simple.

- cocktail shaker
- strainer
- citrus juicer
- muddler
- jigger

GLASSWARE. A great place to start a special glassware collection is at the thrift store. You may even have some incredible pieces passed down through your family. Now remember, you can drink a great cocktail out of a coffee mug if you need to. But keep these on your radar if you want to build your collection (and feel free to mix and match patterns and colors):

- rocks glasses
- highball or tall glasses
- red and white wine glasses
- champagne glasses
- copper mugs
- specialty glasses (margarita, martini, tiki, etc.)

A Secret Weapon for Home Mixologists

If you stock one mixer for your home bar, make it ginger beer. It mixes beautifully with just about any liquor you can imagine and creates a spicy, flavorful cocktail. Mixed with vodka, it becomes a Moscow Mule; with whiskey, a Kentucky Mule. Add ginger beer to gin to mix a Foghorn, or add it to rum for a Dark and Stormy. You can even add a squeeze of lime to create a delicious mocktail. Follow the recipe below to choose your own cocktail adventure.

1. Pour 2 ounces of your liquor of choice over ice.
2. Squeeze in ½ lime.
3. Top with ginger beer (approximately 4 to 5 ounces).

Create a Prism Suncatcher

Spotting a rainbow in the sky almost feels like magic. And you can put some of that magic right in your home in a very simple way, with a prism suncatcher.

This idea is hardly an idea. It's more of a reminder that a very small and simple act can make your space feel special and uplifting. I could launch into a whole lecture on color theory or the psychology and effects of color on the human mind, but I think we both know that seeing something special like a rainbow just plain *feels good*.

YOU'LL NEED:

- Prisms or suncatchers
- Clear string or fishing line
- A sunny window

HOW TO:

1 Find a prism with a hole at the top so that you can thread string through the hole. If you use a clear string or fishing line, the prism will look like it's gently floating.
2 Hang the upper end of your string at the top of your window frame (this is a great instance to use a Command hook).
3 Wait for the sun to shine and enjoy the rainbows!

NOTE: For a different feel, try hanging a disco ball from the ceiling or placing it on a shelf in a sunny spot in your home. Every day when the sun shines on it, you'll have your own personal disco hour.

Craft Faux Floral Words

In elementary school, I used to write little encouraging sticky notes to myself. I would open my binder and find "Today is a great day!" scrawled on a Post-It, waiting there for me. These floral words are kind of like my grown-up version of an encouraging Post-It. An uplifting message to you, from you. And don't be afraid of this simple DIY. It's like everything else you'll find here—easy and attainable but with a beautiful, joyful payoff.

YOU'LL NEED:

- Wire cutters
- Coiled floral wire
- Scissors
- Faux florals and greenery
- Floral tape
- Command hooks

HOW TO:

1. Use your wire cutters to cut off a few feet of wire. Start bending it to form your words. Don't be afraid to really work it into straight lines or curves. Experiment a little with the type of writing you'd like to use. For each word, all of your letters will need to be connected, so think "cursive."

2. Using scissors, cut off a few stems of florals, planning where you'd like them to be. I like the sparse look for this particular project, but you can cover as much or as little of the wire as you like. Cut a stem to 2 to 3 inches long, then place it against a portion of the wire word. Wrap floral tape around and around the stem until the flower is secured against the wire. Rip off the end of the tape.

3. Repeat with more florals. Try fun combinations of flowers and greenery, and place the combinations at various spots along the wires until you're satisfied.

4. Hang on your wall using Command hooks, by hooking them under two looped letters far enough apart to hold the word level.

Medatative Haven

Playful Hideaway

Sexy Space

Refreshing Sanctuary

Set a Bedroom Mood

Good vibes come in a wide spectrum! Maybe the uplifting feelings you need one day are more peaceful and introspective, while the next day you want to feel pumped up and powerful. With some easy tweaks and tricks, a single space can hold all of this and more.

My bedroom has always been a haven for me. As a kid, I would flop down on my beanbag and write my innermost fifth-grade thoughts in my journal while I blasted '90s pop music. In college, my bedroom was host to many wild ideas and creative projects. And now as a mom, I find it a peaceful place to be when I need an energizing reset. What's the vibe in your bedroom? Create the uplifting vibe you need on any day of the week with some of these ideas. Mix and match the pieces that feel right for your space from these lists and watch it transform.

MEDITATIVE HAVEN

CHOOSE FROM THESE . . .

SIGHTS: ☐ plenty of plants ☐ neutral color palette ☐ clear of clutter
☐ filtered lighting ☐ art that brings you peace

SOUNDS: ☐ nature sound playlists ☐ white noise ☐ wind chimes
☐ meditation podcasts | books on tape

TEXTURES: ☐ supportive pillows ☐ yoga mat for stretching
☐ luxurious throw rug ☐ floor cushions or poufs ☐ comfy socks

IDEAS: ☐ peaceful incense or diffuser scents (see pages 43 and 61)
☐ yoga or Pilates videos on your laptop ☐ a small sand garden
☐ things to do with your hands (knitting, drawing, etc.)
☐ a seat with a window view

PLAYFUL HIDEAWAY

CHOOSE FROM THESE . . .

SIGHTS: ☐ your favorite colors everywhere ☐ FaceTime with family
☐ a word game app ☐ souvenirs from your travels on display
☐ a statement wall with a pop of color or pattern

SOUNDS: ☐ your favorite pop music ☐ standup comedy ☐ your best
friend on the phone ☐ vinyl on the record player ☐ your friend's band

TEXTURES: ☐ bright, mismatched pillows ☐ a cool art piece made by
you ☐ fiber art, weavings, or macramé ☐ cozy throw blankets
☐ a mix of vintage and modern pieces

IDEAS: ☐ a tray of your favorite candy on the nightstand ☐ a hanging
chair ☐ flea market treasures ☐ furniture rearranged (see page 127)
☐ surfaces accessorized with your favorite objects

SEXY SPACE

CHOOSE FROM THESE . . .

SIGHTS: ☐ soft lighting ☐ your favorite rom-com on TV ☐ rich jewel
tones ☐ bold art ☐ mirrors to reflect candlelight

SOUNDS: ☐ a sexy curated playlist ☐ a classic jazz album
☐ romance novels on tape ☐ peaceful silence ☐ a small water fountain

TEXTURES: ☐ casual, rumpled bedding with a sumptuous texture
☐ a bed canopy ☐ velvet throw pillows ☐ a soft carpet at the bedside
☐ romantic, flowy curtains

IDEAS: ☐ your favorite candle ☐ a scarf over the lampshade or low
lighting ☐ removable wallpaper in a bold pattern ☐ curvy shapes
☐ a no-phone rule

REFRESHING SANCTUARY

CHOOSE FROM THESE . . .

SIGHTS: ☐ your favorite books ☐ a journal and a pen ☐ family photo albums ☐ unexpected art combinations ☐ flowers on the nightstand

SOUNDS: ☐ the outside breeze ☐ music from childhood ☐ children playing in the yard ☐ a smart speaker with an audio assistant ☐ positive news podcasts

TEXTURES: ☐ blackout curtains ☐ natural art like branches or driftwood ☐ a made bed ☐ a weighted blanket ☐ new knobs and hardware with a fresh finish

IDEAS: ☐ open windows ☐ diffuser with citrus blend (page 62) ☐ clutter-free nightstand drawers ☐ your favorite snack ☐ framed old ticket stubs, maps, or meaningful ephemera

Weave a Wall Hanging

A large part of me wishes I had thought of this idea decades ago so that it could have graced the walls in any of the twelve apartments I've lived in. A woven wall hanging brings so much to a space: texture, color, depth, and a visual treat. Create and style it to be placed above a window as we did in my daughter's room to act as a stand-in for a traditional valance or window treatment. Or add it to any wall for an instant shot of happy vibes.

Weaving newbies, never fear. If you can tie your shoes or braid hair, you've got this covered.

YOU'LL NEED:

- Wooden dowel
- Cotton macramé cord
- Scissors
- Measuring tape
- Cardboard

- Hanging materials (Command hooks or curtain rod hangers)
- Optional: tie-dye kit, trash bag, spray bottle with water

HOW TO:

1 Plan the width of your hanging. If you're making a window valance, make it about 2 inches wider than your window. Cut your dowel to this length.

2 Cut lengths of macramé cord. To determine how long to cut your cords, measure the height that you'd like for your hanging. Double this, and add 5 inches.

3 Attach your cords to the dowel with lark's head knots. To do this, fold a cord in half. Slip the folded end under the dowel and pull the loop so there is a bit of slack. Then insert the two loose ends through the loop and tug to tighten. Repeat until you have cords attached all across the dowel.

4 Hang the dowel on the wall or lay flat on the floor. Smooth and arrange all cords evenly. Then use scissors to trim the ends of the cords into the shape you desire. This could be a chevron, scallops, a diagonal angle—anything you like.

5 To create the tassels on the sides of the hanging, wrap a long section of cord around your cardboard several times (more wraps will create a fuller tassel). Slip a second cord under all of the wrapped cords, and tie a knot to hold them all together. Slip them off of the cardboard. Use a third piece of cord to wrap around all of the pieces about an inch under the top knot, and tie this off to secure. Cut the loops at the bottom and separate the fibers of the cord as desired. Make more tassels and suspend them from the ends of your wall hanging.

6 If desired, dye your hanging. Prepare your favorite tie-dye colors, according to the instructions on your kit. Lay the hanging down on a plastic trash bag in a work area. Spray the areas that you'd like to dye with the water bottle to dampen them. Then, apply tie-dye to these dampened areas. Allow to dry completely.

7 Using Command hooks or curtain rod hangers, hang your weaving and untangle any cords.

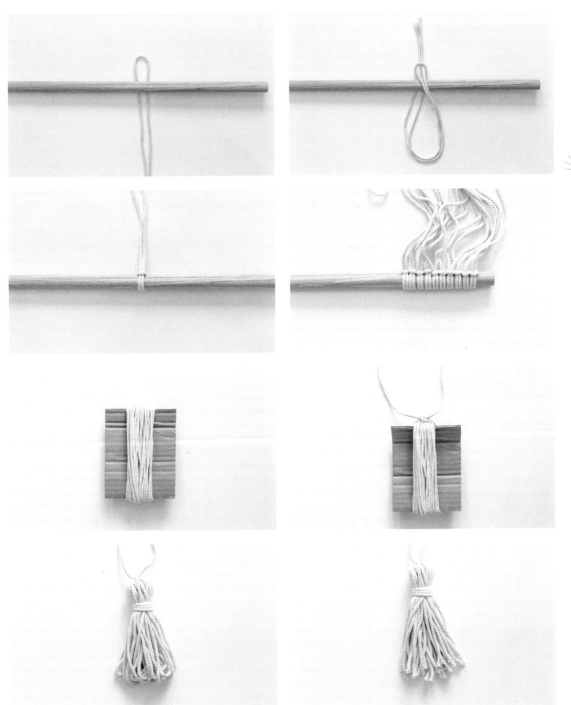

Color-Block Your Walls

I will forever sing the praises of painting a wall! It's one of the most affordable and low-barrier ways to breathe life and joy into a space. A gallon of paint (or, heck, just a quart) and a few hours can truly make a room into something entirely new.

So dream up something that makes you feel wonderful in your space! This color-blocking technique elevates a simple paint job even further by creating blocks of color, rather than painting an entire wall. Use your imagination to create something that's unique to you, or try one of the examples here.

YOU'LL NEED:

- Paint in your preferred colors
- Paintbrushes
- Yardstick
- Pencil
- Painter's tape
- Roller and roller tray
- Optional: butcher paper

HOW TO:

1. If your wall currently has other color on it aside from white, you may want to consider first adding a primer or white coat of paint to prep the wall. This can help you avoid having to paint multiple coats of color later. If you're painting in corners or tight areas like trim and molding, try a thin, angled paintbrush to cleanly paint corners.

2. Decide on the shape of your color block. It could be a diagonally angled block on a wall, a wide, bold stripe around the room, or even rounded shapes. Use the yardstick to measure the area where you'd like to paint, and make light pencil marks on the wall to notate where you will place painter's tape. Make the pencil marks about 12 inches apart across the space you are painting. If you're creating arched shapes, it may be more helpful to cut out the shape from a large piece of butcher paper, tape it on the wall, and trace the shape.

3 Once you have your pencil marks, place lines of painter's tape to connect the marks, ensuring that the tape remains taut and level as you smooth it onto the wall. Stand back every so often to check your progress at a different perspective. Press and smooth the tape into the wall to remove any warps or bubbles.

4 Start painting! Use a clean angled brush to start cutting in your colored paint from any edges that it may abut. (You can mask the edges with painter's tape if you like.) If you have no corners or edges, start by painting over the edges of the painter's tape, which will create the border on your block of color.

5 Now begin rolling out the bulk of your color-blocked section. Load the paint roller with a thin coat of paint and slowly roll it onto the wall in your taped-off area. Follow behind with a brush and get any detailed areas that may be too small to get with a roller.

6 If another coat is necessary to get full coverage, repeat Step 5. Let the paint dry thoroughly.

7 Slowly and carefully pull away the painter's tape to reveal your color-blocked room.

Super-Secret Trick for Clean Paint Lines

To get the edges of your color-blocked paint extra crisp, try this professional painter tip. Once you've applied painter's tape, use a paintbrush to apply a light coat of paint in the same color as your existing wall, covering the edge of the painter's tape, which will be the border of your block of color. This way, any paint that may accidentally seep through or under the painter's tape will be the same color as your wall. The paint then creates a barrier so that the new color won't seep through. You'll see clean edges with no flaws. Be sure to wait for this to completely dry before painting your block of color over it.

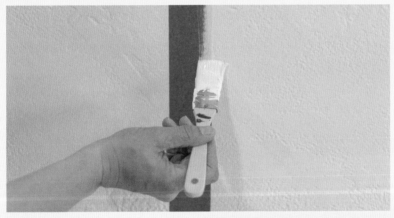

Calm

Make your home a safe and peaceful haven.

Is there a space in your home where you go to retreat? A room that safely keeps the worries of the world at bay while you mindfully regroup? In my home, my safe haven is the bathroom.

Not for nothing, but I'm pretty sure lots of moms of young children would agree that sometimes the only place they can go for five minutes of uninterrupted time is the shower (and even then, those five minutes are often cut short). But the bathroom space that we created in our home is more than just a place to hide. It's steeped in calm feelings, intentionally peaceful design, and organizational happiness.

My favorite shade of yellow brings joy to the room, balanced by a rich blue-green that calls to mind peaceful, deep waters. Beautiful bottles line the shower shelf, creating a harmonious and spa-like feeling. There's a place for everything we need within easy reach and an approachable vibe in the space that makes it feel welcoming rather than stuffy. This is the place where I start and end every day—brushing teeth, putting hair up, wiping off makeup. A place that provides a joyful peace before I go out into the world.

It feels important for a home to have a place like this. You deserve these lovely moments of calm throughout your day, where your home can hold space for you in a way that feels restorative and centering. Perhaps your bathroom is a refuge for you too—or maybe not. Maybe you find this feeling in a bedroom or a den or sprinkled throughout your home. There's no one right way to infuse your home with calming feelings; the right way is the way that feels good to *you*.

And speaking of you, let's talk about your home. Let's dig in with a few stress-free prompts to help you get thinking, writing, and brainstorming about your space. Bring your journal and favorite pen to a place that you love and write down some responses to the questions below. Let it be easy! As you read the prompts, start writing what first comes into your head, and don't belabor your thoughts. Your first instinct is a good one.

FUNCTION

- What are some characteristics of your dwelling that feel calming to you?
- What are some characteristics that feel stressful or chaotic to you?
- Is there anything in your home that doesn't have a home of its own? What objects do you own that seem to be always in the way?
- Imagine you've had a long, challenging week. It's Friday afternoon and you're looking forward to getting home to relax. You walk in the door, drop your keys—where do you go to sit (or lie) down and rest?

  - Why do you choose this place?
  - What does this place hold for you that feels calming?
  - What will you do when you get there?

FORM

- What colors feel peaceful and calming to you?
- What types of textures do you surround yourself with when you want to feel rested?
- What kinds of scents bring you serenity?
- Think of one of your most favorite hotel experiences. Jot down any details that you can remember. Think of anything! Bedding, lighting, the view, the lobby, toiletries, textures, colors, layout, and more.

Pretty Up and Label Your Bottles

We all have our hang-ups, and one of mine is a big, chaotic mess of toiletry bottles in the shower. It may feel like a small thing, but sometimes the little things have a major impact on the way we interact with our spaces.

Give this idea a shot to create a calm, cohesive, and elevated spa vibe in your shower. You can accomplish it in just a few minutes, but the aesthetic shift could bring peace and calm to your everyday.

YOU'LL NEED:

- Clear, reusable toiletry bottles
- Waterproof alphabet stickers
- Toiletries
- Optional: cutting machine and adhesive vinyl

HOW TO:

1 Make a plan for which of your toiletries you'll place in each bottle (use sticky notes if you need help remembering).
2 Use the waterproof alphabet stickers to label each bottle accordingly (some ideas might be shampoo, conditioner, body wash, moisturizer, face wash, lotion, kids' shampoo, etc.).
3 Transfer your toiletries from the mismatched bottles into your new reusable bottles, and recycle the original containers if possible. Next time you need a refill, check for earth-friendly, bottle-free refills, or take your bottles to a refill station if there's one in your area.

NOTES:

- If you have a cutting machine like a Cricut, make your own bottle labels. Simply use the machine's software to create text in a font of your choice, cut it out of adhesive vinyl, and add it to the bottles.
- Use this same technique for the bottles on your bar cart for a pretty and pulled-together effect.

Make Your Own Nontoxic Room Spray

Ditching toxins at home wherever you can is good for you, kids, and pets! If you find that traditional room sprays give you headaches or have a chemical smell, try this lovely and simple nontoxic room spray.

Concoct a scent that's quintessentially *you*, bottle it, and spritz it anywhere when you need to feel calm and centered.

YOU'LL NEED:

- Your favorite essential oils
- Small spray bottle (around 2 ounces)
- Salt (Epsom, Himalayan, or sea salt)
- Distilled water

HOW TO

1 Decide on your essential oil mix. For calming vibes, you could try a floral scent like lavender, a woodsy scent like blue spruce, or spices like nutmeg and cinnamon for a cozy feel.

2 Place 8 to 15 drops of essential oil in your empty spray bottle, depending on how strong you'd like the scent. You can use just one scent or try a blend (find some great blends on page 62).

3 Add a teaspoon of salt to the oil. Allow the oil to somewhat absorb the salt, giving the bottle a shake to mix. Salt acts as an emulsifier to aid in the mixing of the oil and water and ensures even distribution of your essential oil throughout the room spray.

4 Now fill the bottle with distilled water and place the spray bottle cap in place. Shake thoroughly to mix. Spritz the air whenever you need a pick-me-up or calm-me-down scent.

NOTES:

- Be sure to give the bottle a shake before each use to mix the ingredients for optimal scent.
- Change the mood of your space by changing the oils you use. Try citrus oils for energizing scents or herb oils for an earthy, natural vibe. Try any of the oil blends on page 62, or experiment with your own.

Make an Upcycled Matchstick Holder

It's one of my great joys to feel like I've made something special out of something ordinary. There is a sense of pride and ownership in making—a feeling that you definitely won't find in the aisles of a big-box store. To look at your space and see things you have made, serving and supporting you, instills a sense of satisfaction and calm.

I especially love giving new life to things that I would otherwise discard. Aside from the obvious perks (upcycling disrupts consumerism and can save money), it feels exciting to flex our creative muscles and explore the types of things we can make for ourselves. And just the act of making things with our hands connects our physical bodies to our creative minds in a calming and centering way.

This upcycled matchstick holder can start as any small container—a jam jar, an empty jar of face cream, or even a candle. It serves a purpose that aids in the calming routines of lighting candles or incense, so that you can appreciate it each time you use it. Add your own creative twists as you try this simple project.

YOU'LL NEED:

- Empty container, not too large but big enough to hold matches
- Lightweight spackling
- Putty knife or other spreading tool
- Match strike sheet
- Pencil
- Scissors
- Optional: paint or clear glaze

HOW TO:

1 Begin by completely cleaning out your empty container. Wash with warm, soapy water to ensure that any material it held is cleared away and no residue remains. Dry thoroughly.
2 Start adding spackling paste to the sides of the container. Because this material is usually used to patch holes in walls, it's great for building and creating texture. Hold the container by putting the fingers of one hand inside, and use the other hand to spread spackle around it.

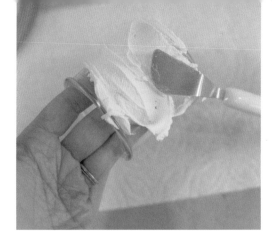

3 Don't overthink the texture. You can create a pattern with the putty knife if you like, but you can also just create a varied texture to give the container an abstract plaster feel.

4 Allow the spackling to fully dry according to the instructions on the packaging.

5 If you like, you can add paint or glaze to your container at this point. (The glaze would give the spackle a glossy look.) You can also choose to leave it plain. If you paint or glaze, allow the layers to fully dry before moving on to the last step.

6 Cut a circle of your match strike sheet to the size of the bottom of your container, using a pencil to trace around the container and then scissors to cut the strike sheet. Flip the container over, remove the backing on the strike sheet to expose the sticky side, and adhere the strike sheet to the bottom. This is where you will strike your matches. Turn the container upright and load it up with matches. You'll always have a match within striking distance when you need to light a favorite candle.

Cleaning a Used Candle Container

If you'd like to use an old candle vessel to store your matches, there's an easy way to clean it. Simply heat some water (a tea kettle works perfectly), and pour it into the used candle. You'll start to see the wax melting and rising to the surface. Use a spoon to remove the wick from the bottom of the vessel and discard. Allow the water to cool completely in the vessel, and as the water cools, the wax will solidify while it floats at the top. Once the wax is solid, remove it, pour out the water, and wipe the inside of the container with a clean cloth.

Calming Scents

If you're burning incense or candles to bring calm to your space, choose a scent that will support your goal. Try some of these aromatherapy tips.

LAVENDER. This may be the most common choice for a relaxing scent and for good reason. Lavender is sometimes considered a natural sleep aid and often used in relaxing environments like spas.

FRANKINCENSE. Often used by aromatherapists to calm anxiety or for meditation, frankincense has an earthy smell with citrus and spice undertones.

JASMINE. The lovely scent of jasmine promotes relaxation, and many aromatherapists use it to foster positive feelings.

PINE. Although often associated with the holidays, a pine scent can bring a calming presence any time of year—especially for someone who loves the outdoors.

PEPPERMINT. The bright, minty scent of peppermint is sometimes used to calm anxious feelings and promote clarity of thought.

VANILLA. The scent of vanilla conjures up thoughts of baking cookies on a cozy day. Try vanilla to spread peaceful and friendly vibes throughout the house.

DIY Incense Holder

Scent has a powerful effect on our moods, creating feelings of calm, tranquility, and relaxation. If candles or diffusers aren't for you, incense can be a soulful substitute. Whereas a candle can take some time to scent an area, incense can work more quickly, and it tends to have a strong perfume and scent throw (meaning that the scent easily travels more distance).

For all of those reasons, I like to burn incense outside in the garden to perfume the backyard. But you can just as easily use it indoors with some safety precautions. Try this handmade incense stick holder in one of your spaces.

YOU'LL NEED:

- Air-dry or oven-bake clay
- Parchment paper
- Rolling pin
- Clay knife or other sharp knife
- Thin straw
- Smooth water glass
- Baking sheet
- Bowls or dishes for molding
- Incense

HOW TO:

1   Start by kneading your clay until it's soft. Then, tear off a sheet of parchment paper about the size of your baking sheet and place it on a flat surface. Using a rolling pin, roll your clay on the parchment paper until it's smooth and even, about ¼ inch thick in all areas.

2   Use your knife to slice your clay into a long rectangle, about 7 x 2 inches. You could also use a rotary cutter or a pizza cutter—whatever you have handy!

3   If you'd like, add some imprints or designs on the clay using the edge of your clay knife or the wrong side of a butter knife. Just gently press the edge into the clay to create stripes or other patterns.

4   Use the straw to punch a hole in the center of the clay. This is where the stick of incense will rest.

5   Trim the parchment paper around the clay so that there's about an inch of extra paper on all sides. Pick up the parchment paper with the clay on it and lay it over the water glass so that the clay creates an arch shape when resting on the glass.

6   If you are using oven-bake clay, place the water glass on a baking sheet, with some small pieces of clay on either side of the glass to hold it in place. Bake according to the instructions on your packaging. If using air-dry clay, simply set the clay aside for a few days until it's completely cured.

7   To make an alternative shape with your incense holder, instead of arching it over a glass, try resting it in an oven-safe dish or bowl. This helps mold your clay into a shape while it's still soft, and the clay will hold the shape once it's cured.

8   Once your clay is firm, insert a piece of incense and enjoy!

Effectively Clear Clutter

For me personally, I know there's nothing that pulls my focus and creates stress in my home space like clutter. It saps my creativity, joy, and focus. In my world, my environment is a physical manifestation of what's inside my head—and if my environment is chaotic, I have a hard time calming my thoughts.

Creating peaceful, calm feelings in a home is often about removing distractions and barriers that stop us from enjoying the space. Then we can allow ourselves the freedom to truly enjoy where we live. And that freedom feels like a breath of fresh air!

If clutter is one of your buzzkills, work your way through this cleanout checklist over the coming weeks or months. Give yourself grace to take it one space at a time, at a pace that feels enjoyable. As you go through each area, clean out the clutter and reorganize if necessary. The goal is to create an environment that feels like it supports you in what you need, gives you space to live, and is filled with your very favorite things.

KITCHEN:
- ☐ cabinets
- ☐ pantry
- ☐ spices
- ☐ refrigerator
- ☐ under sink

BATHROOMS:
- ☐ cabinets
- ☐ medicine cabinets
- ☐ drawers
- ☐ under sink
- ☐ linen closet

LIVING ROOM:
- ☐ media storage
- ☐ cabinets
- ☐ drawers
- ☐ bookshelves

BEDROOMS:
- ☐ closets
- ☐ drawers
- ☐ shelves
- ☐ jewelry box

KIDS' AREAS:

☐ closets

☐ drawers

☐ toy storage

☐ books

HOME OFFICE:

☐ desk

☐ files and folders

☐ cabinets

LAUNDRY ROOM:

☐ cleaning supplies

☐ cabinets

☐ linen closets

GARAGE:

☐ cabinets

☐ drawers

☐ benches

☐ toolbox

☐ trunk and glove compartment of car (your vehicle is an extension of your home!)

OUTDOOR:

☐ storage benches

☐ sheds

☐ closets

If you're having trouble figuring out what to do with specific items, don't worry. It's easy to get overwhelmed, especially if you're a person who has a lot of sentimental items or likes to hang on to things in case you need them "someday." When you get stuck on an item, try mentally (and then physically) putting it into one of three categories: Keep, Donate, or Toss. Use the checklists below to help you sort things out.

KEEP ANYTHING THAT . . .

☐ You still frequently use

☐ Makes you happy

☐ Has significant sentimental value

☐ Has a substantial monetary value (you could decide to sell or donate later)

☐ You use seasonally each year

DONATE ANYTHING THAT . . .

☐ Is in good condition but you no longer use

☐ Doesn't fit (clothing)

☐ You're saving "just in case"

☐ You forgot you had

☐ Is a duplicate of another item you have

TOSS ANYTHING THAT . . .

☐ Can't (or won't realistically) be repaired

☐ Is now digital (instruction manuals, anyone?)

☐ Holds no value for anyone

☐ Is past its expiration date

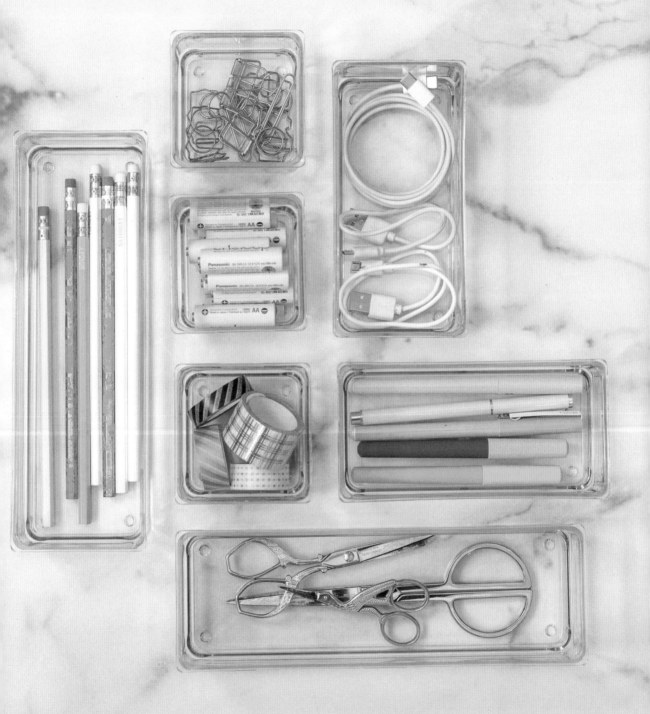

Create an Indoor Herb Garden

One summer we grew basil, and it was the closest I've ever felt to being great in the kitchen. I'm not a cook (although I'm a pretty decent baker). But when I could snip off a batch of fresh leaves (that I grew myself, no less!), layer them with mozzarella and garden tomatoes, and drizzle them with local olive oil, I felt like an absolute pro.

Growing something is special, but growing something that you can cook with is a kind of alchemy you don't often find. Including edible plants in your space can evoke a feeling of peace and calm; some studies show that plants can even increase levels of positivity in humans. Create an indoor herb garden for yourself and see what you can create.

WHAT TO GROW. Grow what you love! Imagine what you would use in cooking or cocktails, and create an herb garden that suits you. Try some of these options:

- **ANNUALS:** Basil, cilantro, chervil, dill, parsley
- **PERENNIALS:** Rosemary, chives, thyme, oregano, mint, lavender
- **ANNUALS VS. PERENNIALS?** Annual herbs live for a single season (or two, in parsley's case). This means that you should harvest these herbs completely by the first frost, as they likely won't survive the winter weather. In some cases, you can keep indoor annuals going throughout the winter months, although the plant and its flavor may weaken. Perennials live multiple years and can survive the winter months with proper care. It's often easier to start a perennial from a cutting of an existing plant, rather than starting from seed, as they can be tricky to start or grow very slowly before they reach a meaningful size.

CONTAINERS. When selecting containers for your herbs, be sure to find pots with drainage so that water can seep through, rather than accumulating in the pot. It's also helpful to plant each herb in its own pot. This provides flexibility for moving things around to get the best light or for replanting should one of the herbs fail.

LIGHT. Indoor herb gardens love a window with a southern exposure—it provides a consistent source of bright but indirect light. If you don't have that, try placing them near an east- or west-facing window. If you see your plants getting tall or leggy with lots of space between the leaves, chances are they're looking for more light. Try using a grow light if you have a particularly dark home.

WATERING. Avoid overwatering; herbs don't love to be overwatered. Keep the soil somewhat moist but not wet; it's even okay to let the soil dry out a bit. Check the soil about an inch under the surface. If it's still very wet, do not water. You may want to try setting a watering schedule to help stay on track. When it's time to water, give them a slow drink to avoid soil erosion around the plants. Once you see water exiting the drainage holes, they've got enough water.

HARVESTING. Pinch or snip off a few leaves or a sprig as needed. Trimming encourages new growth. Avoid harvesting an entire plant at once to keep the plant's growth cycle rotating smoothly.

Energize

I never considered until now how specific the term "living room" is.

After all, until the late nineteenth century, it was called a parlor. A parlor was basically a room for receiving guests or a public space in a home. I'm sure you've also heard the old-fashioned terms *sitting room* (a room for sitting?! Come on!) and *drawing room*—a room where you could *withdraw* to relax in privacy. Those names are well and good, but it feels like they carry a stiffness with them—a certain stuffiness that for most of us faded into the age of corsets and carriages.

But a living room? A room where your life plays out—where you *live?* That's a name I can get behind.

A room that feels lived in is exactly the space I want. Just the thought of that feels welcoming and happy. And the living room in our home is chock full of life, that's for sure. It's a space that feels energized and vibrant, open and bright, and (I sure hope) welcoming to anyone who peeks their head through the front door.

The living room in our home is a gathering space, filled on the daily with a different mix of people and pets, projects and playtimes. This space has been overflowing with the energy of forty cousins at Christmastime and dozens of neighbors for countless summer movie nights. It is late nights on the couch bingeing Netflix, holding sick babies while they sleep. It is stealing the couch cushions to make the perfect pillow fort. It is cocktails with friends, birthdays for Grandma, doing a puzzle for the seventh time. This space, at any given moment, is a snapshot of life. A *living* room.

But if you strip all of those things away, it's just like any other room with four walls and a ceiling. All of that energy, the vibrancy, the joy? That gets baked in by *us*. Lucky you and lucky me, we get to create our homes with intention and purpose and then sprinkle in these beautiful feelings we long to feel.

So how do you energize a space? Well, that's partially up to you (although I do have plenty of ways to help). In my family's case, we created a living room that feels filled with energy from weaving in our favorite things. It brings me joy to see the things I love playing a part in our daily lives when I walk around this space. It's a plain room with white walls, but there are vibrant and surprising colors everywhere. One particular feast for the eyes is a shelf of books organized in an ombre rainbow. Flea-market or side-of-the-road furniture finds have been cleaned up and integrated into the room. Plants grown from cuttings given to us by friends and family are peppered around. Souvenirs from our family travels grace the shelves, along with photos of moments that are written on our hearts.

None of these things are particularly important or sentimental to the people who visit our home, but the joyful and energetic feeling that comes together is still palpable to our guests. Creating a mood in a room may begin with specific objects, but it soon becomes something intangible—you just *feel* it. And perhaps the most beautiful thing of all is that it's not expensive or unattainable or even difficult.

Filling a room with energy and good vibes is just a matter of intention, time, and a little guidance (and I've got you on the guidance part).

Now here comes the juicy stuff! This is the part where we get to talk about *you*. Incredible, complex, unique, extraordinary you. Let's consider your own home and the things you love about it. Also factor in the things that feel not-quite-right, off-balance, or undone. And finally, brainstorm the things that you feel would energize and bring joy to your space. Find a quiet place, get out a favorite notebook or journal that you love, and jot down your thoughts in response to some of these prompts.

FUNCTION

- Where are the pain points or obstacles in your home as you go through everyday life? The stuff that's just plain annoying? These are energy zappers. Think of things like:

  - Objects that are hard to reach or obstructed
  - Items you frequently run out of
  - Things that keep breaking over and over
  - Annoying clutter
  - Things you bump into or knock over

- Now consider a few ways to proactively address your specific obstacles and conserve some mental energy.
- Room by room, consider your storage options. Are you using storage as efficiently as you could be? Might there be a reorganization that could energize a space by making things easier with better flow?
- Are your most-used items the easiest to access in your spaces? Why or why not?

FORM

- Close your eyes and imagine yourself on a day when you feel energetic, hopeful, and happy. What do you look like? Where are you? What are you doing, wearing, seeing? Try to think of as many details as you can.
- Now, imagine how you could bring some of those energetic daydreams into your space. Think of things like:

  - Colors that energize you
  - Aesthetics that feel joyful to you
  - Textures and patterns that uplift
  - Small details, items, or sentimental objects that brighten your day
  - Whether your ideal space is spare or chock full of things

- Which room in your home feels the most energized to you? Why do you think that is?
- Is there a space in your home for which "energetic" would feel like the wrong mood or tone?
- What are some things that make a space (any space, not just your own!) feel energetic to you? Consider all the senses—sight, sound, smell, taste, and touch.

Once you put some thought into these prompts, let your responses guide you through any space in your home that you want to energize. Perhaps your answers will lead you toward a certain project or idea in this book or even spark a fresh idea of your own. Put your pen down and start creating a space that you love.

Arrange a Harmonious and Welcoming Coffee Table

Picture this. A friend stops by say hello. You invite them in for a cup of coffee (or tea, if it's me). While you're brewing it up in the kitchen, they move to the living room to get comfortable. What kind of experience do you want to create for them?

Another scenario! You're working from home and the couch is your office. What could you do with the space to make it as enjoyable and lively as possible?

These are the kinds of questions to ask yourself as you're setting up a coffee table space. I'm not one for a fussy coffee table setup, but I do believe that an intentional and thoughtfully organized area will not only energize your space but also bring a feeling of harmony when you kick your feet up at the end of the day.

Use these tips and tricks while you're arranging a coffee table and enjoy the good vibes they bring.

MAKE IT FUNCTIONAL. It's pointless if you can't *use* it, right? Consider how you use the space and set up accordingly. Include cute coasters if you like to drink around the couch, find a pretty bowl to hold all of your remotes, and make sure to leave some open space to let things breathe (or so that you can actually set things down on it!).

MAKE IT WELCOMING. Include items that could be fun conversation starters—a puzzle, an intriguing book, a sentimental item. These pieces will not just bring you joy but also be a catalyst for conversation with guests.

MAKE IT INTERESTING. Play with height and scale in the pieces you include; try to avoid multiple items of the same height. Also mix various textures like metal, wood, or textiles. Varying all of these things creates visual interest and draws the eye to different items. Remember: if everything looks similar, then nothing feels important!

MORE QUICK TIPS TO TRY

- Add something green; plant life energizes a space immediately.
- When in doubt, remove something! If it feels cluttered, it probably is. Try taking away an item or two to create breathing room.
- Don't forget color!
- Try including a tray or basket for a pulled-together way to hold everyday items.
- Remember the rule of three: decorative items look best grouped in odd numbers.
- Keep in mind that nothing is permanent. Your space is flexible enough to change with your moods and needs, so don't be afraid to mix it up.
- The rule that trumps them all? Use what you love! Make the space feel like *you* and you can't go wrong.

Mix Diffuser Recipes for Every Room and Mood

I believe in the power of scent. Have you ever had a particular scent hit you and trigger a sense memory that you didn't even know was stored in your mind? There's a shampoo I use that brings me right back to some very happy childhood years; I don't particularly like what the shampoo does for my hair, but that scent is worth it for the feeling it evokes.

Scent is a powerful way to change your space and create a feeling for yourself, your family, and your guests. Do you know the feeling of walking into a friend's house and being hit with a heavenly smell? It draws you in, invites you to stay, sets a mood. You can do this in your space for yourself.

Now, I'll be the first to admit that I just scratch the surface in the world of essential oils. I don't use them topically or ingest them, but I do think diffusing oils is a lovely way to scent a home.

There are many ways to diffuse scents. You can use a traditional ultrasonic diffuser, diffuse with reeds, or even just drizzle a cotton ball with your oils and set it in a small dish on the counter. However you choose to diffuse, try one of these energizing and uplifting oil blends throughout your home to brighten your days. I recommend trying one at a time so that the scents are distinguishable and you can identify your favorites.

NOTE: Always practice safe handling of essential oils using our tips on page 64.

LOVELY DAY

Botanical, refreshing, reviving

- 3 drops eucalyptus
- 3 drops rosemary

GOOD MORNING

Bright, natural, invigorating

- 3 drops tangerine
- 1 drop thyme

WALK IN THE WOODS

Outdoorsy, crisp, bracing

- 3 drops bergamot
- 2 drops juniper
- 2 drops cedar

FRESH AIR

Citrusy, fresh, brightening

- 2 drops lemon
- 2 drops mint
- 2 drops grapefruit
- 1 drop lavender

HOME SWEET HOME

Sweet, uplifting, happy

- 4 drops orange
- 2 drops ginger

How to Handle Essential Oils Safely

Essential oils can be a lovely and useful addition to a home. They're a versatile tool to keep around and fun to experiment with. But it's also important to treat oils with care and practice basic safety measures.

1. Read labels. Any time you purchase an essential oil, check the label or packaging for any safety guidelines pertaining to that specific oil. I highly recommend adhering to the manufacturer's recommendations.

2. Know your oils. Rather than play a guessing game when it comes to using or combining oils, do your research about the specific properties of the oils you're interested in. Some are stronger than others, some cause sun or skin sensitivity, and some should be diluted. Treat them accordingly.

3. Dilute. And speaking of dilution, it's handy to keep some fractionated coconut oil handy to dilute stronger oils. It's lightweight, easily absorbed, and a perfect non-greasy carrier oil option. It's recommended to dilute an oil when using it for the first time, using on sensitive skin, or when applying to children. A suggested ratio of one drop of essential oil to five drops of dilution oil is a good place to start; use a 1:10 ratio for stronger oils.

4. Avoid sensitive skin areas. I mainly use oils at home for scents and in my household cleaning, but many enjoy using them topically. If you do, be sure to avoid sensitive areas like the eyes, inner ears, nose, any broken skin, and other areas.

5. Store safely and supervise children. Store your oils in a cool, dark area with the lids tightly capped. Also be sure to store them out of reach of children, and supervise any time your children are near the oils to ensure safe usage. Also keep pets safe from contact with essential oils.

6. Practice sun safety. If you're using oils topically, be aware of which oils will make your skin sensitive to the sun; it's often (but not exclusively) citrus oils. Practice sun safety by avoiding direct sun or UV rays within 12 hours of using these oils topically.

7. Wear gloves if necessary. If you have particularly sensitive skin, you may want to wear gloves when handling essential oils. If the oil comes into contact with your skin, wash the area with soap and water immediately.

8. Ask your doctor. I recommend consulting with your physician before using essential oils if you have any specific questions or concerns.

Assemble a Glass Jar Terrarium

When we started adding more plants to our home, it really came alive. A home filled with plants feels vibrant, lush, and full of life. But we do have one rule for plants in our house—nothing that's too difficult to keep alive! Houseplants shouldn't feel like stress or work, especially because there are so many varieties that are low maintenance.

A terrarium is a fascinating way to grow plants—it's like a little world unto itself. Closed-lid terrariums capture their own condensation, which helps the plants inside survive. And this glass jar terrarium is a perfect upcycling project to create a cozy little home for some lovely plant life. It's a great spot to propagate small clippings. Nurture them as they grow in the jar, and once they outgrow it, they'll be ready for planting in the great outdoors.

YOU'LL NEED:

- Empty glass jar with lid
- Pebbles or gravel
- Activated charcoal (you can find this at a nursery or home improvement store)
- Potting mix (see the soil suggestions on page 76)
- Small plants that like tropical or humid environments (mosses, ferns, peperomia, pilea, etc.)
- Decorative items like tiny figurines, shells, or pretty stones

HOW TO:

1. To the bottom of the jar, add a layer of pebbles or gravel about 1 inch thick. This assists with drainage inside the terrarium.
2. Add a thin layer of charcoal. The charcoal helps absorb any sitting water and helps avoid bacteria buildup.
3. Add a layer of potting soil. This layer should be deep enough to house the roots of your plants, most likely 1 to 2 inches.
4. Nestle your plants into the soil so that the roots are covered.
5. Add any decorative touches.

6   To water your terrarium, simply open it and use a misting bottle to spritz 2 to 3 times with water. Do not pour water into the terrarium. You should never have standing water inside, and you will probably find that you need very little water. If the soil looks completely dry or if the leaves look droopy, it's probably time to water. Place the lid back on top and the moisture and condensation will continue to circulate throughout the terrarium.

7   Closed terrariums like bright but indirect light, so place it in your home accordingly. If you find that condensation collects on the sides, simply remove the lid for 1 to 2 hours. You could also try moving it and giving it a little less light to remove condensation.

Create a Conversation Jar

Sitting around the table at dinner, my family has begun a game called "Highs and Lows." It's not so much a game, I guess, as a way for us to communicate and share with each other in a meaningful way. We go around the table and anybody who wants to will share a high and a low part of their day. (My five-year-old's highs usually feature either recess or candy.)

Perhaps Highs and Lows isn't for everybody. But I love the idea of creating a way to facilitate conversations that become rich and joyful, soulful and telling. And that's how the conversation jar was born.

You don't have to just use a conversation jar around the dinner table (although you sure could!). You can bring it out during cocktails with friends, during time around a fire pit, or over coffee with a bestie. No matter how or when you choose to use it, this easy idea immediately infuses energy and interest into a gathering or a conversation.

YOU'LL NEED:

- Slips of paper
- Pen
- A jar, bowl, or container (if you plan on keeping it out on display, make sure it's a vessel that brings you joy!)

HOW TO:

1 Brainstorm some questions that you think would make interesting or fun conversation.
2 Write one question on each slip of paper.
3 Fold the papers in half and add them to the jar. Repeat until the jar is fairly full.
4 Mix the papers in the jar to make sure the questions come out in random order.
5 During your next gathering or hang, bring out the conversation jar and encourage friends or family to pull a question and chat about their answer.

→

QUESTIONS TO ASK

There are no right or wrong questions to ask in a conversation jar. But to get you going, try some like these.

- What is your favorite color/food/type of music/place/drink/TV show/ etc., and why?
- Where is one place you've traveled that you need to see again? One place you won't return to?
- What is one of your strongest memories from school?
- If you were a beverage/item of clothing/vehicle/etc., what kind would you be, and why?
- Describe a perfect day.
- How did you meet your best friend?
- If you could change somebody's mind about anything, who and what would it be?

MORE THOUGHT STARTERS

- Create conversation jars based on age groups. Make one for your younger elementary-age children, one for high schoolers, one for adults, or one that spans generations.
- Fill the conversation jar not just with heavy or deep questions but also some softballs that could lead to great, lighthearted chats.
- If you get stuck for question ideas, imagine what you would ask family members or friends from generations past.

Draft a Patio-Cleaning Checklist

I have lived in homes where my "outdoor space" was a fire escape suspended above a busy city street, and I have lived in homes where the backyard was so big I didn't know what to do with it. And you know what? They were equally enjoyable.

An outdoor space is what we make it. My guess is that when you welcome guests to your patio or deck, the laughter and happiness that fills it will be the same whether you're on a fire escape or half an acre of manicured lawn. What matters is that *you* love your space—and it'll love you back.

Our outdoor spaces are just begging us to fill them with family, friends, and good memories! They give us life, and you can practically feel yourself becoming energized in the outdoors, just as a droopy plant perks up after being watered. Keeping your patio fresh and ready brings an energy to both your home and your heart.

Every few months, run through a patio-cleaning checklist to make sure that your patio is a place where you truly love to be.

- ☐ CLEAR THE COBWEBS. A quick once-over will keep the area clean and pests at bay.
- ☐ GIVE IT A SWEEP. Sweeping (or blowing, if you have access to a leaf blower) is a superfast way to brighten up an outdoor area.
- ☐ CHECK THE LIGHTS. Every so often, check any exterior bulbs for damage and change any that have burnt out.
- ☐ WIPE DOWN FURNITURE. Keeping patio furniture clean is the easiest way to ensure that the space feels inviting and ready to use.
- ☐ SERVICE THE GRILL. If you have a grill, check the propane level, hose connections, and give the surface a quick scrub.
- ☐ TRIM THE PLANTS. Trim away any dead leaves to keep things looking fresh and encourage new growth.
- ☐ WIPE WINDOWS. If you have windows on your patio, wipe away the grime to make things look sparkly.

Garden in Pots

The first time my kids planted seeds and saw little green shoots peek out of the soil a few weeks later, I'm pretty sure they thought they were wizards. And to be honest, I sort of feel the same when my plants are doing well. To put something in the ground and see those new leaves unfurl every so often feels like magic and gives me life.

Whether your space is large or small, a container garden is a perfect way to start on your journey to becoming a green thumb. Incorporating plants into your home is a simple way to introduce fresh and vibrant energy. Try these easy tips for gardening in pots.

POT AND PLANT SIZE

Selecting a pot that's the right size for your plant will help it thrive. Plants potted in containers that are too small could cause it to become rootbound and stunted. If you're repotting a plant that you purchase, try to pot it in a container that's 2 to 3 inches larger in diameter than the original temporary pot. This will give the plant space to grow and spread out, both above and below the soil.

Be selective as you choose your materials. A grouping of colorful or visually interesting pots can add vibrancy to an area. A selection of bold, colorful flowering plants feels aesthetically refreshing. Choose pieces that feel energizing to you, and your space will reap the benefits.

Choosing Plants That Will Thrive

As you're choosing plants for a container garden, go armed with some information about what will do well in your environment. Before selecting plants, try to have an idea of where you'll keep your container garden. Is it indoor, outdoor, sunny, shady, prone to getting lots of rain? These details will help you select plants that will love the environment. Also, do a quick internet search for your gardening zone on the USDA Plant Hardiness Map. This map will help guide you toward plants that will thrive in your part of the world.

CHOOSING SOIL

As tempting as it might be to scoop some soil from your garden and use it to pot your plants, they'll most likely benefit more from a potting mix. Some potting mixes contain actual soil and some are soilless, which means they contain a mix of organic matter such as peat or wood chips, with perlite or vermiculite to help keep the mix loose and promote drainage. Read the labels on potting mix options to see which would best support the plants you choose.

HOW TO PLANT IN A POT

Fill the bottom of the pot (about one-third to one-half, depending on the size of the root ball on the plant that you're potting) with potting mix. Remove your plant from its previous pot and gently break up the soil and roots to loosen the ball slightly. If you're planting multiple plants in one container, start at the center of the pot with the largest plant and work your way outward, filling around the plants with scoops of soil. Add enough soil so that the base of the plant is covered with soil up to the same level it was in its previous container. Aim to have the surface of the soil about an inch or two below the rim of the pot.

WATERING CONTAINER GARDENS

After planting, water your plants using a gentle setting on a hose nozzle or a watering can. Your watering schedule will depend on the need of your individual plants, but you'll find that plants thrive when you figure out a schedule that they like and really stick to it. If you find that some soil erodes over time due to watering, simply add a few more scoops of soil to the pot to replace it.

Choosing Purposeful Plants

Growing your own herbs is incredibly rewarding (see Create an Indoor Herb Garden on page 49), but there are so many other types of purposeful plants to try. These plants can invigorate your daily routine as you use them in various ways. Here are a few to explore:

- Aloe (healing and medicinal properties)
- Citronella (mosquito repellent)
- Bamboo (edible shoots)
- Lemongrass (medicinal properties and mood elevator)
- Bay leaf (flavorful in recipes)
- Lavender (aromatic)
- Spider plant (natural humidifier and air purifier)

Create a Sunrise Doormat

There's so much opportunity waiting outside our front doors. It's a perfect chance to create a runway for yourself and your visitors, a safe spot to land before you come in and kick up your heels. How do you feel when you walk up to your front door? Do you love what you see? Does that welcoming area reflect what's inside your home?

A cheerful and energizing addition seems like the perfect thing for a front porch, and a sunrise doormat is full of just the right amount of charm to do the job. You almost can't help but smile when you walk up and see that sunshine at your feet. This is an easy but high-impact project that's guaranteed to make your guests smile and put a bounce in your step as you come and go from your safe haven.

ENERGIZE

YOU'LL NEED:

- Natural rectangular doormat (coir with a vinyl backing)
- Pencil
- Box cutter
- Masking tape
- Scrap cardboard
- Outdoor spray paint in your choice of color

HOW TO:

1. Place your mat facedown, and use a pencil to draw an arch on one long edge of it
2. Carefully slice through the rubber on the back of the mat with your box cutter. The fibers on the front will easily come apart.
3. Flip the mat faceup, and use masking tape to create a sun shape. Be creative with the sun rays! They could be thin, thick, short, or extend all the way to the edge of the mat. Continue to mask any areas of the mat that you don't want painted.
4. Place the mat on a piece of scrap cardboard. In a well-ventilated area, apply spray paint according to the instructions on your paint's packaging. Apply one coat to the unmasked areas. If desired, apply another coat for more coverage.
5. Remove the masking tape, and allow the paint to fully dry and cure for at least 24 hours before using the mat.

Comfort

When our daughter was three months old, she caught a respiratory virus. Her little breath sounded like a shrill whistle, and she would stop breathing every so often in her sleep. Those weeks were some of my lowest as a parent. She needed care and attention around the clock, so we set up camp on the living room couch. We would take shifts overnight to hold her so that she could rest, while we nestled in among the cushions, pillows, and blankets.

If you've ever had a sick kid, you know that the nights are the worst. I don't know if it's an old leftover specter of a childhood fear of darkness, or if logically you know that the doctors are all asleep and if something really bad is going down, you'll end up in the emergency room. I would sit with her wheezing on my shoulder and just count down the hours until sunrise.

But somewhere in those blurry days and nights, she started getting better. The wheezing got softer. She strained less for breath. One night I realized that she had been sleeping on me for hours without crying. And through all of those days and nights, somehow our little spot on the couch had become so comforting. It was where our family had gotten through the worst together. A special nest, a little cocoon of reassurance.

Even now, years later, that spot on the couch is where we set up camp with our kids when they're sick.

The comfort that a home can provide is twofold. Obviously, it feels good to be in a home that, well, feels good—soft sheets, a comfy couch, a cozy fireplace. But a home that can comfort both your body *and* your heart, that is a home worth living in. A home that reassures you, that bolsters you, that reflects you. A home that has seen you at your worst and stood in good stead until you were on your feet again.

In our home, creature comforts are everywhere. A weighted blanket for more soothing naps, everybody's most-loved water glasses and tea mugs within easy reach (even and especially for the kids), nightlights to make bedtimes more magical, a candle that smells like a trip to Italy. And it's not just aesthetics that are intentional and considered but also the type of creature comforts that calm my order-loving heart. Drawer dividers that keep bobby pins and toothbrushes in their own lanes. A coat closet where you can see and easily grab everybody's winter gloves. This organizational comfort adds to the feeling of wholeness in our home.

So as you consider *your* home, think of these many modes of comfort. Recognize the role that order versus chaos plays for you in a space. Contemplate the kinds of tangible, physical comforts that speak to you and draw you into a room. And examine your home on the whole, considering the comfort it provides you. Does your house hold a loving space for you in a way that no other place does? Is it your refuge? What ideas or projects might infuse more of that kind of comfort into your home?

FUNCTION

- Which of these statements feels truer for you? Why do you think that is?

  - I feel the most at ease in an environment with structure, systems, and organization.
  - I thrive on the unexpected, unpredictable, and a bit of healthy chaos.

- Do you find yourself losing time to obstacles in your daily routine? Do things like missing items, undone jobs, or distractions send you off track? What other things are time sucks for you?
- Are there any projects in your home that you've been meaning to get to "one day"? What projects, in which rooms?
- Are there any rooms in your home that serve double duty? For instance, a living room that's also a home office, a kids' room that two children share, and so on. What are the challenges about these shared spaces?

- Brainstorm a list of creature comforts that bring you joy. Think big! These could include naps, scents, favorite foods, hot baths, alone time, soft textures, and more.

    - Do you have access to these things in your home? Why or why not?
    - Do these things feel like necessities or like splurges?
    - Where is a place you could infuse some of these into your everyday?

- Build an imaginary perfect room in your home, purely for comfort. What would you put in it? Start with furniture, then decor and art, then any extras you love.
- Do you have any comforting memories of home, either in your own home or someone else's? What comes to mind?
- How could you address each of the senses (smell, sight, sound, touch, taste) in a comforting way in various areas of your home?

As you begin to see patterns in your responses, examine those patterns for clues as to how you could find and create comforting moments in your home. Look through the projects in this chapter (and others as well!) to choose a few that will help you on your way.

Light Up Your Outdoor Space

Have you ever spent an evening outdoors that somehow felt magical? If you have, I'll just bet that there was some kind of twinkly lighting giving you those good vibes. Did you know that some studies show that those twinkle lights can actually produce dopamine, the brain's "feel good" chemical?

Whether it's the dopamine or whether it's the fact that string lights make many people nostalgic for the holidays, adding fun lighting is an easy and fast way to make your outdoor area extra comforting, cozy, and inviting. Up the comfort factor on your patio with one of these quick lighting ideas.

CANDLES. A classic! If you're in a windy area or want to find something you can use over and over, consider faux candles. You could also place candles in tall hurricane jars to keep flames lit in the breeze.

MINI STRING LIGHTS. Wrap these around the backs of furniture, frame outdoor art, or string them through plants or trees.

FAIRY LIGHTS. Wired fairy lights are great for tucking into unexpected places, especially if they're battery powered. Fill clear glass bowls with fairy lights and set them around the patio.

CAFE LIGHTS. If you want to create something more permanent, string round cafe lights in swags across your patio or outdoor area.

LANTERNS. Battery-powered lanterns are easy to bring out in a few seconds flat and handy to store away for next time.

Concoct Fresh + Fragrant Simmering Spices

Have you ever walked into a home that smelled so good it actually made you happy? Perhaps it smelled like baking cookies or fresh flowers or even potpourri. Isn't that the best feeling? As we spend time in our own home, we can become numb to the sights, sounds, and smells that surround us every day. But when we introduce something new and refreshing, it sparks the senses and ups the happiness factor in such a comforting way that you feel wrapped in a bear hug.

Simmering mulling spices on your stovetop is an all-natural, easy, and creative way to scent your entire home. Try some of these seasonal recipes to refresh your home and bring a feeling of peace to your days.

YOU'LL NEED:

- Saucepan or pot
- Water
- A mix of fruits, spices, herbs, and botanicals (see recipes on next page)

HOW TO:

1. Start by filling your saucepan or pot about ⅔ full of water. Place the pot on a back burner on your stove if possible.
2. Sprinkle in the ingredients for your mulling spices. Choose one of the recipes that follow to bring comfort on any given day or season!
3. Turn on the burner to simmer. The spices don't need to be warmed at a high heat; low and slow is ideal. As they start to simmer, you'll smell that wonderful mixture spreading through your home.
4. As your pot simmers, continue replenishing water to ensure that it never completely evaporates while your burner is on. If you notice that the scent has faded while the pot is still simmering, scoop out the mulling spices and add a fresh batch to revive the scent.
5. Once the scent fills your space, turn off the burner and enjoy.

Try these recipes for different seasons or moods.

REFRESH

- 2 lemons, sliced
- 4 sprigs rosemary
- 1 tablespoon vanilla extract

HAPPY

- 3 limes, sliced
- Handful of fresh mint
- 5 sprigs thyme
- 1 inch ginger root, sliced

COZY

- 1 teaspoon pumpkin spice seasoning
- 2 cinnamon sticks
- 1 teaspoon ground nutmeg
- 1 tablespoon vanilla extract
- 1 tablespoon whole cloves

GLOW

- 1 orange, sliced
- 1 apple, sliced
- ½ cup fresh or frozen cranberries
- 2 cinnamon sticks
- 1 tablespoon whole cloves

BRIGHT

- 1 orange peel
- 1 grapefruit peel
- 1 lemon peel
- Handful of fresh mint

HOME

- 1 apple, sliced
- 1 vanilla bean, sliced longways
- 1 tsp almond extract

BREATHE

- 3 fresh pine sprigs
- 1 tsp whole cloves
- 1 tsp whole nutmeg berries
- 4 sprigs rosemary

Whip Up Easy Bathroom Curtains

Creating a bathroom space that you love can be an act of radical self-care. Think of exactly how much time you spend in your bathroom. It's the space that greets us every day as we rub the sleep out of our eyes and prepare to go out into the world. Allowing ourselves to actually enjoy the experience of spending time in the bathroom doesn't have to be a luxury—it can be an everyday feeling.

Layering textures in a bathroom space is a fast and affordable way to make it feel more special, whether you own or rent your home. Try making a set of simple, no-sew bathroom curtains to soften the space and provide some comforting privacy.

YOU'LL NEED:

- Fabric
- Iron
- Curtain rod with hanging clips and accompanying hardware
- Drill or screwdriver
- Measuring tape
- Ruler
- Fabric marker
- Scissors
- Iron-on fabric-fusing tape

HOW TO:

1 Start by choosing your fabric. Look for a fabric with a texture that complements your bathroom. Good choices could be something sheer or flowy or even a linen that hangs nicely. Wash and iron your fabric before cutting.

2 Be sure to choose a curtain rod that's wider than your window. Select a rod that comes with hanging clips so that you can clip your curtains up once they're complete. Hang your curtain rod according to the directions on the packaging, using the included screws and hardware. For a bathroom, it's appropriate to vertically hang the rod 3 to 4 inches above the window frame, and horizontally 3 to 4 inches outside the edges of the frame.

3 Decide where you'd like the fabric to end. You can create short, cafe-style curtains (as seen here), or let them drape to the floor for a more romantic look. Measure from the curtain rod to the point where you'd like your curtains to end; add 2 inches to accommodate a hem—this is your fabric length. Now measure the width of your window; this will be the width of

each of your panels (you want the curtains to be gathered and full, so you will be making *each* panel the width of the window). On a flat surface, lay out your fabric, right side down. Measure and mark the back of your fabric using a ruler and fabric pen or pencil. With sharp scissors, cut two pieces of fabric to these measurements.

4   Now you'll create a simple no-sew hem on all sides of each of your fabric panels. Heat an iron to your fabric's settings. Fold each edge in ½ inch and iron to create a crease.

5   Cut lengths of the fabric-fusing tape and place on the folded edges. Fold these edges over again, keeping the fusing tape inside this fold, and iron again. The fusing tape will hold the fabric together, creating a faux hem. Continue this all the way around both fabric panels.

6   Hang the fabric panels using the curtain clips.

Make a DIY Leather Key Basket

In a sea of crafters and DIY-ers making things that are just for show, I've always been the one who has made things for a *reason*. There is something incredibly satisfying about creating something that's not only beautiful but also truly useful. It feels good to use creativity to solve a problem and serve a purpose.

The purpose served here? A home for things that always go missing. There's nothing more aggravating than realizing you've lost your wallet or keys as you're dashing out the door. Creating a safe and lovely spot for the contents of your pockets is a simple way to bring comfort and ease to your routine.

YOU'LL NEED:

- Leather (real or faux), at least six inches square
- Scissors
- Ruler
- Rag
- Clothespins
- E6000 or another strong, textile-friendly adhesive
- Optional: spray bottle
- Optional: leather finish or sealer

HOW TO:

1. Cut a piece of leather into a square or rectangle, depending on your preference. The piece shown here is eight inches square. Use a ruler to ensure that parallel sides of your shape are the same length as each other.
2. Dampen the leather. To do this, dip a rag in water, squeeze out the excess, and gently spread the water over the leather until it is absorbed. (You could also use a spray bottle to apply a fine mist all over the leather until it's evenly damp in all areas.)
3. Pinch together each corner of the leather and secure individual corners with clothespins. It's important to do this step while the leather is still wet and flexible. Set aside until the leather is completely dry and becomes a bit stiff.
4. Apply a small amount of E6000 in each corner, in between the two pieces of leather being held together by clothespins. Replace the clothespins to hold the corners while the glue dries.
5. After the glue dries, remove the clothespins and give your leather a quick buff with a soft rag. You can also add a leather finish or sealer if you like.

Boost Your Workspace Comfort and Productivity

The aesthetics of a workspace, whether in your home or at the office, have a profound impact on your ability to enjoy the space. But no matter how beautiful it is, a workspace also wants to be outfitted for comfort to be a place that you want to spend time in. There's a balance of form and function to be found, and often they meet at an intersection of the perfect office supplies!

The more comfort and joy we can find in our workplace, the freer we are to find a style of productivity that feels good. I'm actually a fan of productivity but not the style that's often celebrated—the hustle, grind, and constant expectation of doing *more* are not what rings true for me. A mode of productivity that centers around self-care, which asks us what things are truly the most important to us and then helps make space to do those things—*that's* where I live. And that's what you can create for yourself with these ideas.

If this rings true for you, you can lean even more into these ideas by researching Danish hygge (the feeling of creating a warm atmosphere and enjoying the good things in life) and Chinese feng shui (the ancient art of arranging objects and spaces to achieve harmony and balance). Comfort may go by many names in many languages, and yet it's clear that we as humans all seek those same feelings of peace and contentment.

CREATURE COMFORT WORKSPACE SUPPLIES

Make your workplace cozy, comforting, and inviting so that you actually *want* to be there.

SUPPORTIVE SEATING. This may be one place to lean in on function rather than form. While cute desk chairs are fun to look at, you're not looking at the thing—you're sitting in it! Find a comfortable chair that helps alleviate neck or back pain.

HYDRATION. Staying hydrated assists with mental clarity, fatigue reduction, and boosted productivity. Keep a lovely water bottle easily accessible. You can even place a small humidifier on your desk if you're in a dry environment.

WRIST PROTECTION. Jobs that include lots of typing or mouse work can be tough on wrists. Invest in a mousepad, mouse, or keyboard with wrist support to alleviate pain.

CELL PHONE STAND. A cell phone stand helps bring your smartphone up to eye level, next to a computer screen. This can help avoid "tech neck," neck pain resulting from constantly straining to look down at a device.

SPACE HEATER. Hands down, one of the best parts of my workspace is the little space heater hiding under my desk. It's like you're cozied up to a fireplace while you tackle emails.

FOOTREST. A footrest is a brilliant idea for short legs, knee or hip pain, or chairs that aren't quite the right height. Place a small footrest under your desk to create a more comfortable seated configuration.

PRODUCTIVITY SELF-CARE IDEAS

Stop grinding and start enjoying the things you do by incorporating some of these ideas.

SET A TIMER. In the middle of a large project, try setting a work timer. Set it for 25 to 30 minutes, and during that time, focus only on the task at hand. When the time is up, leave your desk to stretch, get a drink, or find some fresh air. Focusing on small chunks of time helps break a project into more approachable sections that don't feel so overwhelming.

DO THE HARD THINGS DURING YOUR BEST HOURS. For a few days, observe your work habits and try to figure out when your "peak" hours are—the hours where you feel your most fresh, creative, and productive. Once you learn your peak hours, try to schedule the tasks that feel the hardest during those hours.

WRITE DOWN GOALS FOR THE DAY. Research shows that when we write something down, it becomes "encoded" in our minds. So once we jot a goal down, it's more likely that we will follow through and take the necessary steps to complete that goal.

KEEP A DISTRACTION DOCUMENT. Keep a small notebook or a running digital document handy at your workspace to quickly write down distracting thoughts. If, as you're trying to focus, a thought comes along to derail you, notate it in your distraction document. Now you can set that thought aside and focus on the task at hand but not worry that you'll forget it entirely.

JUST START. When in doubt, just sit down and start. You've created a lovely and welcoming workspace! Get comfortable there, and get going.

Develop a Sleep Routine

I could read you statistic after statistic about the importance of quality sleep, but my guess is that won't keep either of us from scrolling on our phones way past bedtime. So I have a few other tricks up my sleeve to help you craft a sleep routine that helps you drift off for the best sleep ever.

Consider this a sampler platter of ideas to create a comforting evening as you get ready for sleep—a bedtime buffet, if you will. I'm just serving up, tapas style, a whole mess of tricks to help you hit the hay and get some quality z's.

Go through these checklists and select something to try from each area. If it works for you, keep it in your routine! If it doesn't feel right, exchange it for another idea. Chances are, when you find something that resonates, you'll recognize that feeling of comfort. Sweet dreams.

SIGHT

- Avoid electronics and blue light devices once you start your bedtime routine.
- Try blackout curtains for total darkness.
- If you like sleeping with light, use a low-light (4- or 6-watt) bulb with a warm tone.
- Consider a sleeping mask.

SOUND

- Try listening to a sleep meditation as you drift off.
- Play nature sounds, such as ocean waves, forest scenes, or rain falling.
- If sound bothers you, try sleeping ear plugs.
- Make a sleep playlist with peaceful music.
- Listen to an audiobook or a podcast that lulls you to sleep.

SMELL

- Use a linen spray with soothing botanicals like lavender.
- Diffuse a calming scent like clary sage, which helps calm restless thoughts.
- Before your bedtime routine, light a candle with a floral scent, such as rose, jasmine, or chamomile. Always extinguish a candle before sleep.
- Include any scent that's peaceful or associated with comforting memories for you.

TOUCH

- Find sheets that you absolutely love. Add a mattress topper.
- Keep moisturizer near your bed for a quick hand and foot massage.
- Apply a lip moisturizer.
- Buy a bolster to put under your knees or a body pillow to spoon.
- Invest in a pillow that speaks to your specific needs.

TASTE

- Ask your physician if melatonin (it comes in gummy form!) is a safe option for you.
- Try a cup of decaffeinated tea before bed.
- Enjoy a small, healthy snack if you usually wake up hungry.

HABITS

- Start your bedtime routine at the same time each evening.
- Try a sleep meditation just before nodding off.
- Keep a journal next to your bed to jot down any thoughts that keep you awake.
- Enjoy a calming bath with soothing botanicals, such as lavender oil and Epsom salt.
- Try five minutes of stretching or yoga before bedtime.
- Keep a "device-free zone" in the bedroom for at least an hour prior to sleeping.

Build a Work-from-Anywhere Lap Desk

It's official: working from home is the new working from . . . well, work. As someone who has worked from home for over a decade, I can personally vouch for the fact that it's crucial to create a work-from-home situation that's comfortable, beautiful, and supports your productivity. But this doesn't have to mean a whole room or a devoted office space.

There are days when I do my best work in a window seat. Sometimes I need to work on the couch if I'm caring for a sick kiddo. And some days, it just feels good to work in bed. So a catchall workhorse like this work-from-anywhere lap desk is a total win. This project is a perfect entry-level DIY for anyone who may be shy around tools, and the payoff is twofold: not only is it highly functional, but it's also beautiful and comfortable to boot.

YOU'LL NEED:

- Cutting board or wood slab
- Short furniture legs (4)
- Pencil
- Screws
- Drill or screwdriver
- Optional: furniture leg pads

SELECTING MATERIALS

Using a beautiful cutting board is an affordable and creative way to source a top for your lap desk. Here's what to look for in a cutting board for this project:

- Consider size, shape, and weight. Ensure that it is wide enough to cover your lap, and if you envision sitting with both legs under the lap desk, take measurements to be sure it will suffice. Also ensure that it's deep enough to hold your computer, papers, or whatever else you might need. Finally, look for a board that is fairly light and easy to move around.
- Check that it's thick enough to accommodate a ½-inch screw to hold the legs in place.

- Try to find a cutting board without any holes or wells cut into it.
- Look for one that's visually interesting, with a lovely grain or a cool shape.

Consider these thoughts when you source the legs for your lap desk:

FIND YOUR FAVORITE FINISH. We used a gold metallic finish, but there are lots of options to try.

ENSURE THAT THE LEGS ARE A HEIGHT THAT WILL WORK WELL FOR YOU. If you intend on setting the table over your lap and having the legs rest on the surface where you're sitting, measure to check that the legs will be tall enough.

LOOK FOR DIFFERENT LEG STYLES. There are two- and three-rod hairpin legs, some with embellishments. You could also find a different style of leg entirely. An internet search for "furniture leg sets" will help narrow down your style.

HOW TO:

1   Decide which side of your cutting board will serve as the top of your lap desk. Place the board facedown on a work surface so that the underside is facing upward.
2   Place your legs in the four corners of the underside of the board. Don't attach them just yet; make necessary adjustments as needed to ensure that the legs are where you would like them. Be sure to leave room to thread your own legs through the gap between the desk legs if that's your plan. Once the legs are in place, use your pencil to trace the screw holes in the brackets exactly where they are.
3   Remove all but one of the legs. Align the leg with the hole tracing. Place a screw in the center of the hole and screw it into the cutting board with a drill or screwdriver. Add any additional screws.
4   Repeat with the other three legs. Once the legs are attached, apply furniture pads to the bottom of the legs if they have a base that may damage any surfaces.
5   Wipe down to remove any dust or wood shavings.
6   If you'd like to customize this project even further, embellish the top of your lap desk with some extra flair. Use a stencil and paint, apply a vinyl pattern (see page 151 for ideas), or use paint pens to create a design that's unique to you.

Empower

Build a space that supports your needs.

I was supposed to be a high school teacher. In fact, I was for a while. I taught high school music, and I still to this day adore high school kids and their energy, boldness, and creativity. We spent countless hours together in the choir room making music that still rings in my ears. But to be sure, teaching high school is a world away from what I do now, which is working from home in our creative studio—a space that we built to serve as everything from a photography and styling space to a shared meeting room.

Our home studio used to be a garage—cement floors, dusty beams, and plenty of unseen spiders tucked away in the corners. It was a space that didn't do much for us but a space that we saw had untapped potential to serve our work and our lives in a major way. When we envisioned a studio in this place, we could see it so clearly: crafting supplies organized in easily accessible cabinets, photo props at the ready, a comfortable lounge area for taking meetings, and desk space that looked out onto the backyard where my husband and I could work side by side while we watched the kids play.

This vision came together only because we were thinking of the space in terms of how it could best serve us. We imagined our wildest dreams—working at home and feeling empowered, supported, and bolstered by our workspace. Once we realized that we could dream this way, we applied the same prerequisites to the rest of the house: How can this space support us? Our goals? Our dreams for our family? The dreams of our kids?

Have you ever looked at your home this way?

I love to think of a home as another member of the family that lives in it. A home needs the same love and care that we do. It is there with us and for us as we make memories together. A home is a safe space when we need to retreat from the world, a nest when we are recovering or regrouping, and a launchpad when we are ready to take on another day. So when we are creating our home, it's natural and instinctive to ask of it: how can you help us?

In our home, we don't have chores; we have "family contributions." The kids contribute by emptying the dishwasher, making beds, scrubbing toilets. The adults contribute by cooking meals, paying bills, driving to gymnastics practices. And our home? Our home contributes with well-organized drawers, easy access to toys and supplies, and a blank canvas ready for us to imprint our needs upon.

With some intention and care, you can create a home that is both powerful and empowering, in that it supports you when and how you need it. Let the ideas in this chapter inspire you in your space and lead you to the areas where your home could provide backup for you in a more effective way.

So let's talk about it! Consider your home and all the ways that it makes your life easy, makes your life challenging, or anything in between. Grab your journal, a favorite pen, and take some time to think through the prompts below. Assessing your own space in this way can be challenging; try to see your home through the eyes of someone who is taking it all in for the first time. You could even ask a friend or family member to bounce these ideas around with you.

FUNCTION

- Open a closet or drawer and jot down what you see inside; try not to focus on the items but more the state of the items.

  - How does this space make you feel?
  - Does this space support your daily goals? Why or why not?

- Consider your morning routine and the path you take through your house before you start your day. Are there impediments or challenges throughout this routine? What are they?
- What does your house do best; where is it the most supportive of your efforts and goals?
- What makes you feel empowered in a space? (Some ideas could be aesthetics, organization, comfort, light, colors, favorite objects, necessary supplies, and so on.)

- Room by room, jot down the parts of your dwelling that you absolutely love (a great window or a perfect chair, for example).
- Next to each item, write a few notes about why you love it.
- Room by room, write down the portions of your home that are challenging or you just don't like (for example, a lack of closets or a broken drawer).
- Next to each item, make a notation if it's something that you could personally improve or fix in some way.
- Brainstorm three places or spaces in the world where you have felt powerful or empowered. Do these places have anything in common? Any differences?

Comb through your responses to find similar themes or ideas, and let those themes guide you through any projects that you try in this chapter. Start creating a space that feels supportive and empowering for your everyday.

Hack More Coat Closet Storage and Organization

How's this for a wild statistic: we each spend about two and a half days a year searching for things we've lost, according to a study conducted by Pixie, a smartphone location app. That missing glove? The socks you can't find? Time thieves, all of them.

But if we can empower ourselves by creating spaces in our homes that support our needs, we can turn the tables and use those precious minutes in our day for other things (like mixing a great cocktail or playing another round of Go Fish with the kids).

Start recapturing those minutes with an incredibly simple coat closet organization hack. It's easy enough for the least crafty of us, but it's an extremely efficient solution to a universal problem. No more lost items or overflowing baskets of mismatched castoffs.

YOU'LL NEED:

- Command hooks (use some that are rated for at least a few pounds; you'll need two for every row of winter gear you want to hang up)
- Soft rope or twine
- Clothespins

HOW TO:

1 Hang your Command hooks on the inside of your closet door. Hang two hooks, one on either side of the door at the same level.
2 Cut a length of rope that's about 8 inches longer than the distance between your hooks. Tie a loop on each end, and hook the loops over the Command hooks. Your rope should be suspended between the two hooks.
3 Using clothespins, clip up all of your hats, gloves, scarves, and more. This is also a great place to organize masks or other daily-use items.

BONUS TIP: If you have little kids, create a low rope for them so that they can take out and put away their own items.

Create a Kids' Room That Promotes Independence

The way that children fill up a space, both literally and figuratively, is extraordinary. Parents, caregivers, and anyone who spends time with kids know this to be true. In parenting my own kids, some days have felt as though I'll never know a reality again where they won't need me to tie their shoes, reach for something from a high shelf, or make their seventh snack of the day.

But in their own spaces, we can create a place for children where they feel empowered to be independent (and we can take a step back to let them flourish). With some intentional thought, safe boundaries, and creativity, we can provide kids a place to learn, grow, and discover who they are—right in their own home.

As you're planning changes to your child's room, consider their individuality. Each child is beautifully unique and incredible! But to create a room that promotes independence and empowerment in your kiddo, keep these few things front of mind.

ACCESSIBILITY. Think about how your child uses their room. Do they love to read? Are they all about playing with toys? Do they use their room to study or do homework? Work together with them to talk about all of the things they like to do in their room.

Once you have a broad map of how they use the space, begin to consider what they need access to in order to safely and easily accomplish those things. For younger children, this may mean ensuring that their most-used toys or books are low enough to reach themselves. For others, it could mean tidying up certain spaces so that their supplies are easy to access and organized.

In a space where children can feel in control of their belongings and surroundings, they are empowered to explore and spend time doing what they love best!

SAFETY. A space where we feel safe is one where we feel empowered; this rings true not just for kids but also for all of us. Creating a safe haven in your child's room contributes to their feelings of ease and confidence as they play and spend time there.

There is no exhaustive list of safety measures that a parent can provide for a child. But there are certainly precautions to be taken. Secure furniture to walls. Ensure that toys are age-appropriate for little ones. Be mindful of exposed outlets or sharp corners. For older children, you may want to consider technology boundaries to protect their mental well-being.

This is a perfect time to consult a pediatrician if you're interested in learning about more ways to create a safe space in your child's room.

COMFORT. As adults, we have the ability and resources to create a space that feels good to us. We can create comfort for ourselves. But our kids don't necessarily have that autonomy. So as you're considering your child's room, talk with them about how you could work together to make it feel like a comfortable and enjoyable sanctuary.

Analyze the space with them again, focusing on how they like to use it. You could create a cozy reading nook for bookworms or a highly functional desk area for older kids. Perhaps it's a drafty room and it could use a basket of lovely, soft blankets.

Our son's room got oven-hot in the summer until we realized he needed some window coverings that kept out the heat. After that, it was so much more comfortable for him to spend time there.

Taking a bit of time to show children that their comfort is as important as ours can communicate respect, show care, and help to create a space that they love.

Make Rope Baskets for Bathroom Storage

By now you might be noticing that lots of the projects and ideas about empowering your space are about organizing, prepping, or otherwise making arrangements in your home so that the space does some of the heavy lifting in your life *for you*. Doesn't that sound lovely? A home that is tailored to your exact needs? That's what empowering your home is all about.

You know what doesn't feel powerful? Bathroom drawers and cabinets that are overflowing with loose bobby pins, brushes full of hair, empty product bottles, and other sad flotsam. Adding a bit of thoughtful organization is a simple way to feel good about your space and let it serve and support you.

Now, you could absolutely run out and grab a few plastic containers to do this job. But this project is a more creative and personalized take on getting your bathroom gear together. These pretty rope baskets are lovely enough to display and strong enough to wrangle your supplies.

YOU'LL NEED:

- ⅜-inch cotton cord (about 15 to 20 yards, depending on how many baskets you'd like to make)
- Glue gun and glue sticks
- Scissors

HOW TO:

1   Decide on the shape of your basket. If you'd like a round basket, fold about 1 inch of rope over onto itself, and glue the tail in place using a hot-glue gun. If you'd like an oval basket, fold over about 4 inches of rope onto itself and glue together. This will be the bottom center of your basket.

2   Continue to coil the rope around itself, creating a pinwheel shape, hot-gluing the rope to itself as you go. This should result in a basket base that continues to grow larger, either in a circle or an oval.

3   Once the base of your rope coil is the diameter that you would like your basket to be, begin working your rope in an upward spiral. Place a few inches of hot glue on your coiled base, and a spiral of rope upward to create the sides of your basket. Press this new piece of rope into the hot glue to affix. Continue working around and up in this manner until you reach your desired height.

4   If you'd like, add handles to your basket. Leave a 4- to 5-inch section of rope unglued and slightly loose to provide some slack. Then glue it down a few inches away, depending on how wide you'd like your handles. Glue and coil the same rope around to the other side of your basket and repeat. Glue the end down and trim any excess.

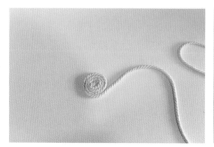
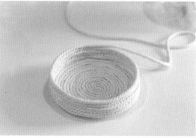

Dress Your Desk

When you sit down at your workspace, how do you feel? Equipped, prepared, powerful? Or is it more along the lines of disheveled, haphazard, and hesitant?

There is such power held in a space that supports your needs. And such strength in building a space like that for yourself. A simple space like a desk can do so many things for us, whether we work from home or in an office. It's where great ideas are born and executed, where we showcase the best of ourselves and do the work that fulfills us. A desk space that makes you feel excited to be sitting at is a gift I wish I could give to every person I know.

Take a moment to think about what inspires you as you do your work. The aesthetics of a space have a major effect not just on our mental state but also our productivity and work satisfaction. Ask yourself a few questions and jot your thoughts down in a journal to start digging into the type of workspace that reflects your deeper needs.

THOUGHT STARTERS

- What items are essential to you as you work?
- What colors do you gravitate toward in your work wardrobe?
- If you could work anywhere else in the world for a day, where would it be and why?
- Do you prefer a bustling, noisy environment or a quiet, peaceful zone?
- How would your colleagues describe you to a new friend?

Let your responses guide you in a direction as you dress your desk. Try one of these aesthetics or mix and match what feels right. The beauty is that no matter the type of space you have, you can incorporate the style or pieces that work for you.

→

NATURAL. Peaceful vibes, neutral colors, and the feeling of bringing the outdoors in. Try dressing your desk with:

☐ a plant ☐ stone textures ☐ crystals ☐ a rattan basket
☐ natural elements

BOLD. Strong patterns, major contrast, and a feeling of power. Try dressing your desk with:

☐ strongly contrasting colors like black and white ☐ bold art
☐ a statement sculpture ☐ metallics ☐ clean lines

VIBRANT. Colorful pops, playful details, and a feeling of lightheartedness. Try dressing your desk with:

☐ bright desk accessories ☐ vibrant florals ☐ inspiring books
☐ interesting colors ☐ fun desk toys

Natural

Bold

Paint a Brick Fireplace

Painting our brick fireplace may have been one of the most controversial projects I ever tackled. About 50 percent of my friends and family were fully on board, and the other half pretty much told me I was ruining our home. Luckily that's never stopped me before, and it didn't stop me this time.

Yes, painting brick is a major commitment. Technically you can reverse it if you decide you don't like it, but it takes a massive amount of time and effort to do that. The good news is, I would paint our fireplace over and over because I loved the result so much.

Painting a brick fireplace is a doable and affordable way to make a massive change in your home's aesthetic. It creates a modern look and can refresh your whole space, bringing a light and bright feel into an area that might have been previously drab or dark. And while it seems like a daunting task, it's easy enough that even home improvement newbies can tackle it. It's an incredibly satisfying and empowering feeling to step back and see the change that you've created in your space.

YOU'LL NEED:

- Supplies for cleaning (bristle brush, soapy water, sponges, rags)
- Painter's tape
- Drop cloths
- Paintbrushes (one flat, one angled)
- Primer or masonry paint
- Interior paint in your preferred color and finish (I recommend eggshell)

HOW TO:

1 Thoroughly clean your brick using some warm soapy water and a bristle brush. Dip the brush into the water and work it onto the brick in a circular scrubbing motion. The goal is to remove as much soot, grime, and gunk as possible. After scrubbing, use a sponge to soak up any excess water. Wring out the sponge, rinse with clean water, and wipe the area. Let it all dry completely overnight. The cleaner you can get your surface, the more effective your paint will be.

2   Use painter's tape to mask any areas you want to remain unpainted. Pay special attention to the area where the brick meets the wall, floor, and mantel (if you have one). Cover the floor with drop cloths to protect it.

3   Apply primer or masonry paint using the flat paintbrush, or the angled brush on edges and corners. This layer helps coat any past soot stains or other gunk on the brick, sealing it in so that it won't seep through the paint. It also helps create a base for paint to stick to and provides color coverage. When applying the primer, be sure that you get it in every single nook and cranny—you really want to prime and seal every area for a successful and long-lasting paint job.

4   If necessary, repeat with another primer coat. If the first coat didn't quite cover all of the brick, it's best to add another coat of primer and avoid multiple coats of paint.

5   Add a coat of your regular paint. You'll most likely end up applying two coats of regular paint to get full coverage and to get a little more sheen from the eggshell finish. The primer is quite flat, and if it peeks through the paint, you may see a contrast in the finish.

6   After two coats, allow the paint to fully dry and assess whether you need a third to achieve full coverage.

7   After your final coat, slowly and carefully remove the painter's tape and allow the fireplace to dry and cure for at least 48 hours before placing anything on the brick surface. (See more painting tips on page 27.)

More Ways to Paint a Fireplace

On this fireplace, the brick responded best when we brushed on the paint. However, different brick may take paint better from a roller or even from a paint sprayer. Try a test patch to see which is the easiest for your fireplace and which makes the most sense in your home setting.

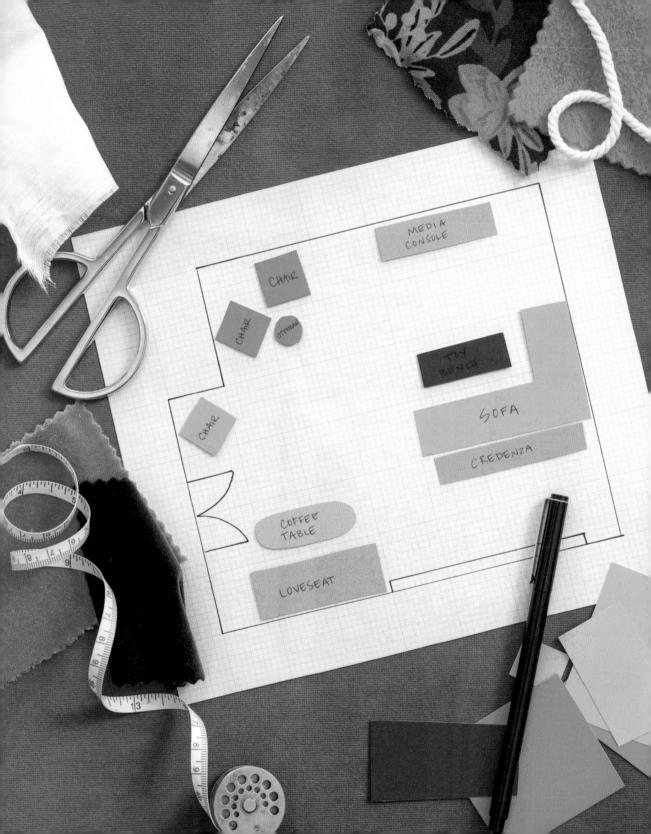

Refresh a Room with a Furniture Reorganization

I'm a self-confessed serial reorganizer. I've been known to change rooms around frequently just for the fun of it. There is a legendary story in my family of the time that my sister and I moved me and all my belongings and furniture from our shared bedroom to the playroom down the hall while my dad was napping. She was twelve; I was eight.

I think that I love the act of reorganizing a space because it's a no-cost way to feel like you have something completely new. It breathes life into your home. You have the opportunity to explore a room in a new way and decide if something different from the norm could possibly suit or serve you more completely. It's a very empowering feeling to fit the pieces of your puzzle together and see your space come to life in a fresh format.

VISUALIZE A FURNITURE REORGANIZATION

Before you start shifting things around, start by visualizing a new layout of the space. There are plenty of online tools that you can use to digitally mock up your space and your furniture, which is definitely helpful when you're visualizing a reorganization. But I always use a very old-school way of planning a room layout: good old graph paper.

Measure out your space wall to wall, and measure your furniture as well. Plot it out on graph paper, creating it to scale (a ratio I often use is two graphing squares for every foot of physical space, so that one square represents 6 inches). Then, plot out your furniture on another piece of graph paper, also to scale, and cut the furniture pieces out. Now you have a miniature version of your room for trying out various furniture arrangements.

TIP: When it comes time to move your real furniture, use furniture sliders to help with moving heavy pieces safely across the floor.

$\longrightarrow$

START WITH ANCHOR PIECES

When planning a furniture layout or reorganization, start with the pieces around which you want to plan the space. Perhaps you have a couch that only fits in a couple of areas or a great carpet that you know you want to use. Maybe your anchor piece is a favorite art print or your comfiest chair.

Whatever your anchor pieces may be, begin your design by positioning those first. Let them help dictate the rest of the space when it comes to furniture arrangement, color palette, layers of texture, and so on.

USE WHAT YOU HAVE

A space doesn't need thousands of dollars of new *stuff* to feel fresh. Creativity goes a long way, both in terms of staying within a budget *and* making a home that feels special, intentional, and curated. Before you shop, use what you have and experiment with how it could be reimagined.

REPAIR. If you have a lovely piece that's in disrepair, explore fixing it first. Reupholster an ottoman, recane a chair, stitch fabric, clean smudges. Give new life to what you already have.

REPURPOSE. Go shopping in your own home! Try putting an item in a new place or using it in a new way. Serving bowls or platters can move to a coffee side table to wrangle keys or display objects. Mirrors can become trays. Move baskets, books, and tchotchkes around and give them a new purpose.

REDESIGN. Small changes or improvements can make an old item entirely fresh. Some ways to switch things up are a coat of paint, new fabric, wood stain, adhesive vinyl sheets, new drawer pulls or knobs, etching—the list goes on. Consider your possessions a starting point and reimagine what they could be with a little creativity.

Express

When people visit our home, I think about half of them enjoy—or are at least intrigued by—the aesthetics. There are wild pops of color around corners like our bright yellow laundry room cabinets, bold patterns like the giant banana leaf wallpaper in the kitchen, and unexpected knickknacks and mementos sprinkled throughout a bright, light space.

I think the other half of the people who visit don't quite know what to make of it.

It's true that our home doesn't look like any other home in the neighborhood. I've had visitors tell me things like, "It's just so . . . interesting!" Sometimes they mean that in a good way, and sometimes they don't know what else to say.

The funny thing is, our house wouldn't stand out an inch on Pinterest, and it would pale in comparison to the pages of a design magazine. We don't have any particularly groundbreaking decor or any avant-garde aesthetics. What we *do* have is a home that takes risks in the sense that we look to ourselves, and not to trend, to decide what we like. We also happen to live in a place where traditional aesthetics are the norm and where anything veering slightly away from that is out of the ordinary. And that's okay!

But when someone comes into our home and says something more along the lines of, "I don't even know where to begin to make my home look like this," I can start to see that they're interested in steering away from those traditional aesthetics. There's just one crucial thing to understand. No two homes *should* look just the same. Because no two people or families or households are the same.

Of all of the feelings that a home can foster and amplify, the satisfaction of self-expression may be the most important to me. The opportunity to take an empty white box of a room, work on it for a while, and make it reflect what's inside you is so gratifying, so exciting, so artful and personal. So when someone tells me they want their home to look similar to mine, what I really hear is something like: *I see you reflected in this space, and I want to see myself in my own space.*

This desire to see oneself in a space is a perfect and pure place to start. You don't have to start with money or loads of time or even an excess of creativity. Start with the desire, and layer on top of it a clarity around the things that you love, value, and treasure. These are the ingredients for creating a space where you will see yourself reflected, a space that feels expressive and happy and intrinsically you. A key component of expressing yourself is gaining that clarity, taking the time to truly know what you like and dislike, and understanding the things that feel important enough to you to include in your home.

As you work your way through these questions and prompts, I have two final cents to add: *let it be easy.* Nobody knows you like you, and nobody can do what you can do. Trust your gut while you jot down the answers that feel the truest for you, and let those answers serve not as rigid rules but as friendly arrows helping to point you in a direction to explore.

FUNCTION

- Consider form versus function within your home. Is there one that weighs more heavily for you or feels more important?
- When you walk into a new place or someone else's home, what are some of the first things you notice?
- What do you think people notice when they walk into your home? If your friends or family had to describe your home, how do you think they would describe it?
- What types of events do you like hosting best in your home? (Intimate meals, large parties, holidays, cocktail hours, sleepovers, meetings?)

    - What makes your home best suited for hosting these types of events?
    - What about your home makes these events challenging?

- Imagine you could fill a suitcase with your favorite or most important possessions. What would you put in it and why?
- What were your favorite outfits to wear as a kid? A teen? In your twenties? What do you remember about these clothes and why you loved them?
- Describe a room that you would walk into and absolutely cringe. Then describe one that you'd walk into and want to live in.
- Let's play *"would you rather."* For each pair below, choose a preference and jot down what it might look like in your home.

  - Bold or subtle
  - Classic or modern
  - Light + bright or dark + cozy
  - Colorful or neutral

Now that you've got some responses helping to guide the way, use them to lead you toward the projects in this chapter that resonate with you. There's no wrong way to add your unique point of view in your home, so enjoy expressing yourself!

Upcycle Wall Art

A bare wall is just begging for something to fill it! Adding art to your walls is prime territory for self-expression; it's a chance to saturate your space with your unique perspective and style. I love to hear people talk about what they hang on their walls and the why behind their choices.

Whether it's something that has been passed down throughout family generations, a piece collected on a memorable trip, or something that simply caught your eye, the art you display fills your space with a sense of who you are. And while there's plenty of collector-level art that is most likely out of the average person's budget, there are many ways to add art to your walls for just a few dollars.

You can find beautiful things to frame in unexpected places. If you're stuck, try some of these ideas.

- OLD CALENDARS with interesting or beautiful art are perfect for displaying. Cut out and frame your favorite image, or create a gallery wall by framing multiple pages from the same calendar.
- GREETING CARDS can be a great place to find affordable (or free, if it's a card that you've been gifted!) art. Frame a greeting card in a frame with an oversized mat to make the piece look even more elevated.
- MAGAZINES, especially ones printed on matte paper, are a major source of inspiring art. Find two or three pages that have complementary images and hang them in multiple frames to create a diptych or triptych.
- GO HUNTING AT A LOCAL THRIFT STORE for interesting art that could be reframed, updated, or personalized in some way.
- KEEP AN EYE OUT AT YARD SALES for art or frames. This is a great place to get large-scale pieces at a fraction of their usual cost. Ask the owner if the art has a story; often you'll learn something incredible about it that makes you love it even more. And if you see a great frame with art that you don't love, you can use it to frame something else.

Create Grid Photo Wallpaper for Your Cabinets

I can't think of a more joyful way to express yourself in your space than filling it with your most treasured photos. Research has shown that displaying photos that we love in our home provides daily positive reinforcement for our brains as we recall our social bonds and how they enhance our lives. In one study by the CEWE Group, the subjects who looked through photo memories felt more nostalgic, happy, and relaxed.

In these modern times, our happy memories often only live digitally in our smartphones. But pulling them off of the phone and into real life is a perfect way to pack our homes with self-expression and good vibes. This project is an unexpected and extra-fun way to display lots of your favorite photos so that they greet you every single day.

YOU'LL NEED:

- Measuring tape
- Pen
- Digital photos
- Online printing software
- Scissors
- Command Strips or double-sided mounting tape

HOW TO:

1. Take measurements of the interior back wall of the cabinet that you'd like to line with photos. This could be the back of a hutch, kitchen cabinets, or a bookcase. Measure the width and height.

2. Get your photos printed. Do an online search for a printing company that creates poster-size photo collages. Upload your images to the site, and organize them as you would like them to print. Be sure you order enough posters to cover the inside of your cabinet backing, based on your measurements.

3. Once your printed posters arrive, cut them to the size of the back wall of your cabinet. If necessary, you may need to join more than one poster to cover the area.

4. If necessary, remove any shelving in the cabinet. Apply Command strips or double-sided mounting tape to the back of your photo posters. I recommend

not just applying these to the edges of the posters but evenly spreading them throughout the center as well. This helps to avoid any sagging.

5   Starting at the top, adhere your poster to the back wall of your cabinet. Align it with the upper corner and continue to adhere it to the wall as you work your way down. Go slowly and check alignment as you go.

6   Repeat if needed with other sections of the poster. Once the back wall is covered with photos, replace your shelving and fill the cabinet with your belongings. Try using this treatment elsewhere, such as at the back of your bookshelves or even on the interior of a closet door.

Style Your Bookshelf

We take such joy in the things that we have accumulated over the years. The things you come home and live with every day, the things that hold memory and meaning.

Give yourself the lovely and simple gift of actively enjoying the objects you own. Bring them out, dust them off, and display them proudly. Mix and match any of these bookshelf styling ideas to infuse some of your uniqueness into your surroundings.

But first, a few general rules of thumb when styling a bookshelf:

- Place your larger objects first; they act as anchors and reference points.
- Next, add in books and/or smaller items, with anything tall toward the back of a shelf and layering the shorter objects toward the front.
- Play with various book arrangements, from standard leaning rows to stacks (bonus points for objects layered on top of book stacks).
- Group odd numbers of items together.
- Layer various textures throughout.
- Stand back and edit! If it feels cluttered, whittle it down to your favorites.

PEACEFUL ZONE

Make your bookshelves into a peaceful haven with neutral or monochromatic tones, simple styling, and plenty of plants.

Try:
- Hiding cords or unsightly items in a textured basket
- Adding lighting with a lamp or sconce
- Making it practical, with containers for often-used items like glasses or pens
- Storing books with spines hidden (a highly controversial idea) to create a monochrome look
- Removing the dust jackets from books
- Creating a mix of large and small items for visual balance
- Tucking in a diffuser or scented item
- Adding life with plants

HAPPY VIBES

Infuse happiness into your space with some bright pops of color, unexpected arrangements, and objects that make you smile.

Try:
- Adding colorful dried flowers for a natural touch
- Exhibiting fun finds from a thrift or vintage store
- Stacking your books in unexpected ways
- Displaying your most colorful objects
- Hanging art in a fresh way (use your Command Strips!)
- Organizing by color
- Displaying collections in groupings, like globes or glass figurines

NOSTALGIC FEELS

Weave in extra self-expression by displaying your most sentimental possessions and prized items.

Try:

- Displaying items from your childhood, including your favorite books from your early years
- Framing favorite photos
- Organizing by timeline or when you collected your items
- Grouping your favorite books together
- Displaying your kids' artwork or old writing
- Creating a theme for your bookshelf, such as travel or animals
- Setting out family heirlooms

Display Kids' Art

The number of times that I've had to sneakily slip my kids' adorable art into the trash is beyond what I can count. Do I love that art? Absolutely! And I'm sure if you're a parent or guardian to a tiny artist, you love their art too. But if I kept every handprint snowman that came home from school, I wouldn't have any place to store my clothes. I mean, the sheer volume these kids turn out is staggering!

What's a mom to do? Their little crestfallen faces when they see their art becoming trash is too much to take. In our home, we came up with a system that serves two purposes: it not only wrangles all of the art but also empowers the kids to choose the art they love best and want to display. Seeing them express themselves and take charge in this way can be a game changer. Try this idea with your kids to help them express their inner artist.

CLIPBOARD GALLERY

YOU'LL NEED:

- Clipboards
- Command hooks
- Optional: adhesive vinyl or stickers
- Kid art

HOW TO:

1. If you like, you can decorate your clipboards before you hang them. Adding adhesive vinyl designs can elevate the look of the whole display and make it feel pulled together. Some ideas could be stripes, polka dots, or organic shapes.
2. Use Command hooks to hang an arrangement of clipboards in an open wall space. Be creative with your placement; try a grid, a straight line, a grouping, or any gallery style that suits you.
3. Allow your kids to place their art on the clipboards as they wish! When they want to hang a new piece, retire the one it's replacing.

One Outdoor Space, Many Ways

I love visiting other people's homes. I love to look around and take in what's important to them, to see how their households work, and to spend time in a space that they've created. Our homes are as varied and individualistic as we ourselves are; no two are the same and I think that's pretty extraordinary.

We shape our homes for many reasons. For function, so that they can be the workhorses we need. For our children, to create a loving, safe, joyful place for them to grow. For self-expression, so that when we look at our home, we see glimpses of our own uniqueness reflected back at us.

We can even shift and alter a singular space over time to accommodate our shifting needs, our possessions, or our aesthetics. Here is a look at a single outdoor space and a few inspiring ways to make it your own.

KID-FRIENDLY

If your reality includes kids, young or old, try some ideas to keep them entertained while also keeping your space feeling enjoyable for the adults.

- DESIGNATE A CREATIVE AREA. Drop a playmat or drop cloth on any areas that need protecting and include some creative ways for kids to get messy. An outdoor easel, a set of watercolors, some air-dry modeling clay, bubbles—these are all great outdoor activities that can keep kids busy while the adults chat.
- HIDE THE MESS. Wrangle kids' toys and gear in pretty baskets to keep everyone happy. This makes for easy accessibility for the kiddos, but cleanup is also a snap when you just toss everything back in. An aesthetically pleasing basket keeps the area from looking chaotic.
- GIVE THEM SEATING. Kid-friendly seating will make them feel welcome in the space and give you a chance to breathe. For younger kids, this could be mini chairs or a comfy chair swing. For older kids, a hammock or lounge is a cool place to read and relax.

CHILL ZONE

For an outdoor space that feels like your own personal oasis, add touches that introduce a major chill vibe.

- BRING THE INDOORS OUTSIDE. Think of comfy textures, pillows, blankets, and places you'd want to relax in. Add colorful throw pillows to a bench, or toss a soft blanket over your chairs. An indoor-outdoor rug can make the space feel extra inviting, along with some charming lighting (try one of the lighting ideas on page 86).
- ENGAGE ALL THE SENSES. Think of all five senses and accommodate them all. Add a small speaker to play your favorite chill music. Try a relaxing diffuser recipe (page 61) or some incense (page 43). Keep snacks and drinks within easy reach. All of these considerations make a welcoming space that you and your guests won't want to leave.
- ADD WALLS. Or faux walls, to be more precise! One way to make an outdoor space feel extra inviting is to make it feel like a semi-enclosed, special spot. Hang curtain panels, position a screen, or try creating a green wall along one or two sides of the space.

FULLY FUNCTIONAL

Creating a functional (and fun!) outdoor space that you can use year-round takes a bit of forethought and a bit of creativity.

- CONSIDER THE SHADE. While you're creating your patio space, keep an eye on the areas where the sunlight hits the strongest. Do your best to shade the important areas (like lounge or eating areas) to keep yourself comfortable year-round. Umbrellas, sunshades, and plants are all great options.
- ADD STORAGE. Make sure to consider storage for all of your backyard gear. Try a bench that doubles as storage and seating, or outdoor ottomans with storage inside.
- DINE OUTDOORS. Dining al fresco is extra special, especially if you have a great place to do it. Create a space in your patio area where you and yours can easily head outside for a meal. A patio table can be a centerpiece or visual anchor for your outside area, providing a place to eat, drink, play games, and talk long into the evening.

Use Decals to Create Faux Wallpaper

I've learned the hard way too many times that wallpaper, while beautiful and lots of fun, always comes to a bitter end when you're tired of it. I can't tell you how many hours I've spent scraping wallpaper (even, sometimes, the kind that's supposed to be able to peel right off).

But there are plenty of ways to avoid finding yourself with a scraper and a sore arm! Peel-and-stick vinyl designs are so varied, colorful, and interesting that the possibilities are literally endless these days. If you have a cutting machine like a Cricut, you can create your own. And if not, you can do a quick search for vinyl wall decals on Etsy to find more amazing options than you can imagine.

Use wall-friendly vinyl decals to create a fun pattern or an abstract design on your walls with this faux wallpaper hack. It's budget-friendly, renter-friendly (it would totally transform a dorm room!), and will infuse a whole lot of personality into your space.

YOU'LL NEED:

- Vinyl wall decals (or removable adhesive vinyl and a cutting machine)
- Cloths
- Soapy water
- Yardstick or measuring tape
- Pencil
- Plastic scraper tool (or something similar such as a ruler or library card)

HOW TO:

1 Read the instructions on your specific packaging if you've purchased vinyl wall decals, as some applications may differ from others. Generally speaking, following the process below will yield a great result.

2 Clean your walls. If you create a clean slate without any grime or residue, your vinyl wall decals will adhere more cleanly to the area. Wipe down the walls with a cloth and warm, soapy water (dish soap will do). Follow with another wipe down using a new cloth soaked in plain warm water to remove any soap residue. Allow to dry or wipe down with a dry cloth.

3 Next, plan your design. If you're planning something very specific and aligned (for instance, rows of pattern), measure your full wall space and

plan out your placement. It can also be helpful to graph this out on a sheet of paper before you dive in. Similarly, if you are planning a more organic placement that is not necessarily a pattern, it's helpful to sketch it out on paper for general placement before you start applying to the wall.

4   Use your yardstick or measuring tape to plot the placement of your decals along the wall, making a light pencil mark for each decal. Be sure you know where that mark should fall on your decals (top, middle, bottom, right side, left side, etc.).

5   Begin placing your decals. It often works best to peel away a corner of the decal first, leaving most of it on its backing. Place this corner on the wall and smooth the rest of the decal down onto the wall as you simultaneously peel away the remainder of the backing. This can often help avoid air bubbles or wrinkles.

6   If you happen to get a bubble, use the scraper tool to gently push the bubble to the edge of the decal. It's also possible to carefully peel up an edge of the decal to straighten it out and reapply.

7   Continue applying decals in your pattern until the wall is complete.

Wrapping Up

A home holds so many things for the people who live in it. It contains our stories, joys, challenges, missteps, triumphs, and everything in between. If our walls could talk, they would brag on us for the many times we've lovingly patched the paint or mended what needed fixing. They would console our children over a skinned knee or a broken heart. And they would laugh out loud with us as we tell jokes around the table with friends.

Your home can be exactly what you make it, and I hope you use this book as a catalyst of inspiration and encouragement to create a space that feels *just like you*. Continue your efforts to view your home with continually fresh eyes, and give your energy to the places that need it. Infuse it with joy, comfort, and all of the little things that make you happy to come home.

Because at the end of the day, it's your home that faithfully waits there for you, to give you a space in which to grow. And I hope that as you grow, you continue to create a home in which you can live your happiest life.

Acknowledgments

Bringing this book to life has been a joy from day one, mostly because of the village that helped along the way. I owe thanks to so many people.

To my editor, Jen Worick, and the Sasquatch team, thank you for seeing the value in this idea, for endless encouragement, and for guiding me through the process with beautiful insight. Working together on *Happy Home* has been a dream.

Incredible gratitude to my management team at Jabber Haus; your tireless work and support are so appreciated.

To Joy Cho, for lending your brilliant voice to this project with a beautiful foreword. Your generosity is remarkable, and your joyful work has paved the way for so many creative women.

Special and heartfelt thanks to *Lovely Indeed* readers, who have been giving me a reason to create for over a decade. You are why I get to do what I do.

To the brilliant women in my life: my sister, my mom, Sandy, Besto B., Katie B., Daley P., Jackie G., Allie S., Jill R., Jae S., Kelly M., and many more. You have cared for our kids, given your time, shared your insights, cheered me on, and filled our home with happy moments that sustain us.

To my mentors: Polly, Daniel, Karen, Candy, and Debbie. Your support of my endeavors means more than you could ever know. Thank you for teaching me many different ways to be creative.

To my dad, who helped us build our happy home, and my mom, who showed me the magic of making.

Henry and Maggie, thank you for being the best photo assistants, for asking how many words I wrote every day, and for inspiring me with your wild creativity.

And to Ryan: I wouldn't have done it without you, literally and figuratively. Thank you for the extra work hours, the photos, and the endless brainstorm sessions. Most of all, thank you for always encouraging me to take up space.

ACKNOWLEDGMENTS

As you are creating your own Happy Home, find inspiration with some of these resources. You'll find everything you need to create handmade projects, furnish a room, add personality to your space, or just get a refreshed vision for your home. Enjoy browsing for treasures, ideas, and inspiration at some of my most frequented sites.

CRAFT SUPPLIES
- Joann.com
- Etsy.com
- Amazon.com

HOME DECOR
- Anthropologie.com
- Bonjourfete.com
- Westelm.com
- Ikea.com
- Etsy.com
- Homegoods.com
- Blinds.com
- Rugs.com
- Crateandkids.com
- Target.com

WALL ART / PHOTO PRINTING
- Annshen.com
- Ariellevey.com
- Society6.com
- Minted.com
- artifactuprising.com

PLANT SUPPLIES AND INFORMATION
- Terrain.com
- Happyhappyhouseplant.com

FURNITURE
- Article.com
- Livingspaces.com
- Nuggetcomfort.com

FEATURED PAINT COLORS
- Behr Paint in Plantain Chip
- Behr Paint in Sherbet Fruit
- Behr Paint in Ocean Abyss
- Behr Paint in Polar Bear

Index

Page numbers in *italic* refer to photographs.

B

Basket for Keys, Leather, *94,* 95
Baskets for Bathroom Storage, Rope,
　117–118, *118, 119*
bathroom, 31
　Easy Bathroom Curtains, 91–92, *93*
　Pretty Up and Label Bottles, 34, *35*
　Rope Baskets for Bathroom Storage,
　　117–118, *118, 119*
bedroom
　Kids' Room That Promotes
　　Independence, *114,* 115–116
　Set a Mood for, *16,* 17–19
　Sleep Routine, *100,* 101–102
Bookshelf, Style Your, *140,* 141–143, *142,*
　143
Bottles, Pretty Up and Label, 34, *35*
Bouquets, Forage, *6, 7*
Brick Fireplace, Painting, 123–124, *125*

C

Cabinets, Grid Photo Wallpaper for,
　138–139, *139*
calming spaces and projects, 29–51
candle container, used, cleaning, 40
children. *See* kids
Clutter, Clearing, 45–46, *47*
Coat Closet Storage and Organization,
　112, 113
cocktails. *See* Home Bar, Stock Your
Coffee Table, Harmonious and
　Welcoming, *58,* 59–60
Color-Block Walls, *24,* 25–27, *27*
comforting spaces and projects, 81–105
Conversation Jar, 69–70, *71*
Curtains, Easy Bathroom, 91–92, *93*

D

declutter. *See* Clutter, Clearing
desks. *See* workspace
Diffuser Recipes for Every Room and
　Mood, 61–62, *61, 63*
Doormat, Sunrise, *78, 79*

E

empowering spaces and projects, 107–129

energizing spaces and projects, 53–79

equipment, xii–xiii

essential oils. *See* scents

expressive spaces and projects, 131–152

F

Fireplace, Brick, Painting, 123–124, *125*

flowers

Faux Floral Words, 14, *15*

Forage Bouquets, 6, *7*

homemade cut-plant preservative, 6

Furniture Reorganization, *126*, 127–128, *129*

G

Garden, Indoor Herb, *48*, 49–50, *51*

Garden in Pots, *74*, 75–77, *77*

H

happiness, in your home, xi–xi

Herb Garden, Indoor, *48*, 49–50, *51*

Home Bar, Stock Your, *8*, 9–11, *11*

home office. *See* workspace

I

Incense Holder, DIY, *42*, 43–44, *44*

J

Jar, Conversation, 69–70, *71*

K

Key Basket, Leather, DIY, *94*, 95

kids

Display Kids' Art, 144, *145*

Kids' Room That Promotes Independence, *114*, 115–116

Outdoor Space for, *146*, 147

kitchen, 3–4

L

Leather Key Basket, DIY, *94*, 95

Light Up Outdoor Spaces, 86, *87*

living room, 55–56

M

Matchstick Holder, Upcycled, *38*, 39–40, *40*

mixer for home bar, 11

O

outdoor space

Kid-Friendly, Chill, or Functional vibe for, *146*, 147–149, *148*, *149*

Lighting Up, 86, *87*

Patio-Cleaning Checklist, *72*, 73

P

painting
  Brick Fireplace, 123–124, *125*
  Color-Block Walls, *24*, 25–27, *27*
  trick for clean paint lines, 27
  Patio-Cleaning Checklist, *72*, 73
plants
  See also flowers
  choosing, 75, 77
  Garden in Pots, *74*, 75–77, *77*
  Glass Jar Terrarium, *66*, 67–68, *68*
  Indoor Herb Garden, *48*, 49–50, *51*
  Prism Suncatcher, 12, *13*

R

Reorganization, Furniture, *126*, 127–128, *129*
Room Spray, Nontoxic, *36*, 37
Rope Baskets for Bathroom Storage, 117–118, *118, 119*

S

scents
  calming, 41
  Diffuser Recipes for Every Room and Mood, 61–62, *61, 63*
  DIY Incense Holder for, *42*, 43–44, *44*
  Fresh + Fragrant Simmering Spices, *88*, 89–90
  Nontoxic Room Spray, *36*, 37
  safety tips for essential oils, 64
  Sleep Routine, *100*, 101–102
  Spices, Simmering, Fresh + Fragrant, *88*, 89–90
  Spray, Nontoxic Room, *36*, 37

storage
  Clear Clutter, 45–46, *47*
  Coat Closet Storage and Organization, 112, *113*
  Leather Key Basket, *94*, 95
  Rope Baskets for Bathroom Storage, 117–118, *118, 119*
  Suncatcher, Prism, 12, *13*
  Sunrise Doormat, *78*, 79

T

Terrarium, Glass Jar, *66*, 67–68, *68*
Toiletry Bottles, Pretty Up and Label, 34, *35*
tools, xii–xiii

U

uplifting spaces and projects, 1–27

W

Wall Art, Upcycle, 136, *137*
Wall Hanging, Weave a, *20*, 21–22, *22, 23*
Wallpaper, Decals to Create Faux, *150*, 151–152
Wallpaper for Cabinets, Grid Photo, 138–139, *139*
Words, Faux Floral, 14, *15*
workspace
  Dress Your Desk, *120*, 121–122, *122*
  Work-from-Anywhere Lap Desk, 103–104, *105*
  Workspace Comfort and Productivity, *96*, 97–99

For Ryan, Henry, and Mags—you are my happiest home, wherever we are.

Printed in China

SASQUATCH BOOKS with colophon is a registered trademark of Penguin Random House LLC

27 26 25 24 23   9 8 7 6 5 4 3 2 1

Editor: Jen Worick
Production editor: Peggy Gannon
Photographer: Chelsea Foy
Designer: Tony Ong

Library of Congress Cataloging-in-Publication Data
Names: Foy, Chelsea, author. | Cho, Joy, writer of foreword.
Title: The happy home : the ultimate guide to creating a home that brings
   you joy / Chelsea Foy ; foreword by Joy Cho.
Description: Seattle : Sasquatch Books, [2023] | Includes index.
Identifiers: LCCN 2022025257 (print) | LCCN 2022025258 (ebook) | ISBN
   9781632174611 (hardcover) | ISBN 9781632174628 (epub)
Subjects: LCSH: Interior decoration–Psychological aspects.
Classification: LCC NK2113 .F64 2023 (print) | LCC NK2113 (ebook) | DDC
   747--dc23/eng/20220719
LC record available at https://lccn.loc.gov/2022025257
LC ebook record available at https://lccn.loc.gov/2022025258

Disclaimer: Unless instructed otherwise, never use essential oil on your skin without diluting it first. Keep essential oils out of reach of children and pets.

ISBN: 978-1-63217-461-1

Sasquatch Books
1325 Fourth Avenue, Suite 1025
Seattle, WA 98101
SasquatchBooks.com